MW01040341

DISCOVERING CAREERS FOR YOUR FUTURE

transportation

Ferguson Publishing Company
Chicago, Illinois

Carol Yehling
Editor

Beth Adler, Herman Adler Design Group
Cover design

Carol Yehling
Interior design

Bonnie Needham
Proofreader

Library of Congress Cataloging-in-Publication Data

Discovering careers for your future. Transportation.
      p. cm.
  Includes index.
  ISBN 0-89434-399-8
1. Transportation—Vocational guidance—Juvenile literature. [1. Transportation—Vocational guidance.
2. Vocational guidance.] I. Title: Transportation. II. Ferguson Publishing Company.

HE152 .D57 2001
388'.023'73—dc21

                    2001033080

Published and distributed by
Ferguson Publishing Company
200 West Jackson Boulevard, 7th Floor
Chicago, Illinois 60606
800-306-9941
www.fergpubco.com

Copyright © 2002 Ferguson Publishing Company
ISBN 0-89434-399-8

Printed in the United States of America
Y-9

Table of Contents

Introduction 1
Air Traffic Controllers 6
Aircraft Mechanics 10
Airplane Dispatchers 14
Automobile Service Technicians 18
Automotive Industry Workers 22
Avionics Technicians 26
Bicycle Mechanics 30
Diesel Mechanics 34
Industrial Traffic Managers 38
Locomotive Engineers 42
Marine Engineers 46
Marine Services Technicians 50
Pilots 54
Public Transportation Operators 58
Railroad Conductors 62
Reservation and Ticket Agents 66
Signal Mechanics 70
Toll Collectors 74
Traffic Engineers 78
Truck Drivers 82
Glossary 86
Index of Job Titles 90
Transportation on the Web 92

Introduction

You may not have decided yet what you want to be in the future. And you don't have to decide right away. You do know that right now you are interested in transportation. Do any of the statements below describe you? If so, you may want to begin thinking about what a career in transportation might mean for you.

___My favorite class in school is shop.
___One of my hobbies is collecting and building model airplanes/trains/ships/cars.
___I would like to get my pilot's license.
___I enjoy learning about trains and railroads.
___I am interested in how motors work.
___I like to help my parents/friends repair their cars.
___I enjoy sailing and being on the water.
___I am interested in traveling to different parts of the country and the world.
___I can't wait to get my driver's license.
___I enjoy reading about people who sail around the world or make long solo airplane or hot-air balloon trips.
___My favorite vacations are cross-country road trips with my family.

Discovering Careers for Your Future: Transportation is a book about careers in transportation, from air traffic controllers to truck drivers. Transportation workers include those who drive road vehicles, airplanes, ships, and trains. They are also the people who build and repair cars, trucks, trains, ships, and planes, as well as those who manage traffic.

This book describes many possibilities for future careers in transportation. Read through it and see how the different careers are connected. For example, if you are interested in air transportation, you will want to read the chapters on Air Traffic Controllers, Aircraft Mechanics, Airplane Dispatchers, Avionics Technicians, and Pilots. If you are interested in road vehicles, you will want to read the chapters on Auto Service Technicians, Auto Industry Workers, Bicycle Mechanics, Diesel Mechanics, and Truck Drivers. Go ahead and explore!

What do transportation workers do?

The first section of each chapter begins with a heading such as "What Diesel Mechanics Do" or "What Traffic Engineers Do." It tells what it's like to work at this job. It describes typical responsibilities and assignments. You will find out about working conditions. Which transportation workers spend most of their time traveling? Which ones work in shops and factories? This section answers all these questions.

How do I get into a transportation career?

The section called "Education and Training" tells you what schooling you need for employment in each job—a high school diploma, training at a junior college, a college degree, or more. It also talks about on-the-job training that you could expect to receive after you're hired, and whether or not you must complete an apprenticeship program.

How much do transportation workers earn?

The "Earnings" section gives the average salary figures for the job described in the chapter. These figures give you a general idea of how much money people with this job can make. Keep in mind that many people really earn more or less than the amounts given here because actual salaries depend on many different things, such as the size of the company, the location of the company, and the amount of education, training, and experience you have. Generally, but not always, bigger companies located in major cities pay more than smaller ones in smaller cities and towns, and people with more education, training, and experience earn more. Also remember that these figures are current averages. They will probably be different by the time you are ready to enter the workforce.

What will the future be like for transportation workers?

The "Outlook" section discusses the employment outlook for the career: whether the total number of people employed in this career will increase or decrease in the coming years and whether jobs in this field will be easy or hard to find. These predictions are based on economic conditions, the size and makeup of the population, foreign competition, and new technology. Terms such as "faster than the average," "about as fast as the average," and "slower than the average," are terms used by the U.S. Department of Labor to describe job growth predicted by government data.

Keep in mind that these predictions are general statements. No one knows for sure what the future will be like. Also remember that the employment outlook is a general statement about an industry and does not necessarily apply to everyone. A determined and talented person may be able to find a job in an industry or career with the worst kind of outlook. And a person without ambition and the proper training will find it difficult to find a job in even a booming industry or career field.

Where can I find more information?

Each chapter includes a sidebar called "For More Info." It lists organizations that you can contact to find out more about the field and careers in the field. You will find names, addresses, phone numbers, and Web sites.

Extras

Every chapter has a few extras. There are photos that show transportation workers in action. There are sidebars and notes on ways to explore the field, related jobs, fun facts, profiles of people in the field, or lists of Web sites and books that might be helpful. At the end of the book you will find a glossary and an index. The glossary gives brief definitions of words that relate to education, career training, or employment that you may be unfamiliar with. The index includes all the job titles mentioned in the book. It is followed by a list of general transportation Web sites.

It's not too soon to think about your future. We hope you discover several possible career choices. Happy hunting!

Air Traffic Controllers

Types of Controllers

Arrival controllers regulate the flow of traffic entering an airspace, establish holding patterns, and clear planes for landing.

Departure controllers coordinate the flow of traffic leaving the airport's airspace.

En route specialists coordinate the flow of traffic between airports' airspaces.

Flight data and clearance delivery specialists receive and communicate flight plans, airport weather conditions, and other data between pilots and other air traffic control towers along routes.

Ground controllers maintain the smooth flow of traffic along an airport's taxiways leading to the runways.

Local controllers speak directly to pilots, prepare them for takeoff, and guide them on the final landing approach.

What Air Traffic Controllers Do

Air traffic controllers use radar and eyesight to watch planes on the ground and in the air to make sure they stay at safe distances from each other. They give pilots instructions and navigation information. They are often called the traffic cops of the skies.

Some air traffic controllers work in the airport tower. They watch all the airplanes as they enter and leave the airport. Usually, more than one controller watches each plane. *Ground controllers* direct planes to the correct runway when they are ready to take off. *Local controllers* keep the pilot up-to-date on weather conditions and clear the plane for takeoff. Once the pilot begins to take off, the plane is guided out of the airport by *departure controllers.*

Landing airplanes are handled in the same way. Pilots radio arrival controllers

IBM

Air traffic controllers monitor the flight patterns of planes on a radar screen.

in the airport tower to notify them that they are ready to land. Controllers check radar screens to make sure there are no other planes in the same general location. Once a runway clears, controllers give the pilot permission to land. After the plane has landed, ground controllers direct the plane down runways until it can approach an arrival gate.

Some air traffic controllers work at en route centers located throughout the country. These controllers keep track of planes during flight. All air traffic controllers have the flight plans of each of the planes they are watching so they know where the planes are supposed to go and

EXPLORING

Visit an air traffic control center. Talking with air traffic controllers and watching them work will provide you with a good introduction to their day-to-day activities. Visits and interviews can be arranged through most airports, air traffic control centers, the Air Traffic Control Association, and many airlines.

can alert the pilot if the plane flies off course or if another plane flies into its airspace. There are strict regulations about how close one plane can get to another, and the air traffic controller's main duty is to make sure that each plane has enough space around it.

Education and Training

You must have a high school diploma to become an air traffic controller. Then you must complete four years of college or at least three years of work experience or a combination of both.

Trainees for controller positions are chosen from applicants who score high on the federal civil service examination. They go through a one-week screening to make sure they have the qualities they need to work under extreme pressure. They must pass physical and psychological examinations and computer simulation tests. Those who pass this screening process train in a seven-month program at the FAA Academy in Oklahoma City. About half of the applicants who start the program are eventually accepted as air traffic controllers.

Controllers are tested about every six months to make sure they are up to date on all the correct procedures. In addition, air traffic controllers also have to pass a physical examination every year, including a drug test.

Earnings

According to the U.S. Department of Labor, the average salary for air traffic controllers was $48,300 in 1999. Salaries ranged from $36,640 to $87,210 a year. Experience, job responsibilities, and the complexity of the facility are factors that influence pay. Controllers with a great deal of seniority and those at the nation's busiest airports can earn more than $100,000 a year in wages, overtime, and benefits. Controllers may also earn bonuses based on performance.

FOR MORE INFO

Air Traffic Control Association
2300 Clarendon Boulevard, Suite 711
Arlington, VA 22201
http://www.atca.org/index.html

Federal Aviation Administration
Office of Personnel and Training
800 Independence Avenue, SW
Washington, DC 20591
202-366-4000
http://www.faa.gov

**National Association of
Air Traffic Specialists**
11303 Amherst Avenue, Suite 4
Wheaton, MD 20902
301-933-6228
http://www.naats.org

Outlook

Competition for air traffic control positions is strong. The U.S. Department of Labor predicts little or no change in the job outlook through 2008. The FAA is currently not hiring air traffic controllers, and many more qualified applicants are always attracted to the job than there are positions available.

Global Positioning System technology is changing the role of air traffic controllers. It gives pilots a far more accurate picture of their position in the sky and allows them to break away from the traditional air routes and chart their own courses. The result is faster and more economical flights. More widespread use of GPS equipment may mean a far more limited role for air traffic controllers, especially en route controllers.

Aircraft Mechanics

What Aircraft Mechanics Do

Aircraft mechanics repair, inspect, and maintain all kinds of aircraft and aircraft engines. Some aircraft mechanics work only on the engine. Others work on the airframe, which is all of the parts of the aircraft except the engine, and some mechanics work on all parts of the plane. Aircraft mechanics adjust instruments; inspect and repair pneumatic, hydraulic, and electrical wiring systems; clean screens; grease moving parts; and check brakes.

Aircraft mechanics who work on airplanes at airports between flights are called *line mechanics.* Line mechanics must be able to work on all parts of the plane. Their main duties include making emergency repairs and doing simple routine inspections and maintenance. For instance, they inspect for oil leaks, check the plane's surface and tires for damage or signs of wear, and test the radio, radar, and lighting equipment. Other tasks are

Overhaul mechanics who work on engines do inspection, maintenance, and repair work. They examine engines for cracked cylinders, oil leaks, and breaks in turbine blades. If necessary, they remove the engine from the aircraft, take it apart, and use special instruments and equipment to detect wear or damage. They replace or repair worn or damaged parts, reassemble the engine, and put it back in the plane.

An aircraft mechanic tightens bolts on an engine before it is installed in a plane.

American Airlines

changing coils, cleaning spark plugs, and refilling hydraulic and oxygen systems.

Mechanics who do periodic scheduled maintenance on airplanes are called *overhaul mechanics.* They usually work at an airline's main overhaul center, and they usually specialize on either the engine or the airframe.

EXPLORING

• Working with electronics kits, tinkering with automobile engines, and assembling model airplanes are good hobbies for future aircraft mechanics.

• Take a guided tour of an airfield to get a good view of the overall work done in the aircraft and airline industry.

• You may earn a student pilot license at the age of 16.

Overhaul mechanics who work on airframes inspect the sheet-metal surfaces, measure the tightness of control cables, or check for rust, distortion, and cracks in the body and wings. *Airframe mechanics* repair, replace, and assemble parts of the airframe using welding equipment, rivet guns, and air or electric drills.

Education and Training

Aircraft mechanics must be high school graduates. High school courses in mathematics, physics, chemistry, machine shop, auto mechanics, and electrical shop will be helpful.

Most aircraft mechanics who work on private or commercial aircraft must be licensed by the Federal Aviation Administration. Mechanics without licenses must be supervised by those who are licensed. Most aircraft mechanics get their training either in the military or in special aircraft mechanic schools that are approved by the federal government.

WORDS TO LEARN

Airframe: The wings, fuselage, tail assembly, and the fuel and oil tanks of the airplane.

Domicile, or base: Airline hangar space used to repair that airline's aircraft.

Fixed base operations: Service facilities offering maintenance services as well as fuel and parking.

Fuselage: The body of the airplane.

Power plant: The aircraft's engines and propellers.

Terminal: An airline's place of business at an airport where planes are docked, passengers and cargo are loaded and unloaded, and basic repairs are made.

Walkaround: A quick inspection of the plane before a scheduled flight.

Aircraft mechanics need better-than-average strength and agility for lifting and climbing. They also must not be afraid of heights, since they must work on the wings and bodies of large jet planes.

Earnings

Some aircraft mechanics, especially at the entry level and at small businesses, earn little more than the minimum wage ($5.15 an hour). The median annual income for aircraft mechanics was about $38,000 in 1998 according to the U.S. Department of Labor. Salaries ranged from $24,700 to more than $52,000 a year. Mechanics with airframe and powerplant certification earn more than uncertified mechanics.

Outlook

Employment opportunities for aircraft mechanics should grow about as fast as the average through 2008, according to the U.S. Department of Labor. The demand for air travel and the numbers of aircraft created are

FOR MORE INFO

Aeronautical Repair Station Association
121 North Henry
Alexandria, VA 22314
703-739-9543
http://www.arsa.org

Air Line Employees Association
6520 South Cicero Avenue
Bedford Park, IL 60638
708-563-9999

Professional Aviation Maintenance Association
1707 H Street, NW, Suite 700
Washington, DC 20006-3915
202-730-0260
http://www.pama.org

expected to increase due to population growth and rising incomes. Job prospects will vary according to the type of employer. There will be less competition for jobs at smaller commuter and regional airlines, Federal Aviation Administration repair stations, and in general aviation.

Airplane Dispatchers

What Airplane Dispatchers Do

Airplane dispatchers, sometimes called *flight superintendents,* are employed by commercial airlines. Their work is not the same as that of air traffic controllers, who are employees of the federal government. They give the airline company's clearance for each flight that takes off. They watch current weather conditions, weather forecasts, wind speed and direction, and other information. Before flights, they decide whether the airplane crew should report to the field or whether the airline should begin notifying passengers that their flight will be delayed or canceled or will take an alternate route

Pilots confer with dispatchers to determine the best route to use, the amount of fuel to be placed aboard the aircraft, the altitudes at which to fly, and the approximate flying time. The pilot and the dispatcher must agree on the conditions of the flight, and both have the option of delaying or canceling flights if conditions are too hazardous to ensure a safe trip.

Dispatchers may also be responsible for maintaining records and for determining the weight and balance of the aircraft after loading. They must be certain that all their decisions are in keeping with the safety regulations of the FAA, as well as with the rules established by their own airline.

Once the planes are in the air, dispatchers keep in constant contact with the flight crews. A dispatcher may be responsible for communications with as many as 10 or 12 flights at one time. Following each flight, the pilot checks with the dispatcher for a debriefing. In the debriefing, the pilot tells the dispatcher about the weather encountered in the air and other conditions related to the flight. The dispatcher uses this information in scheduling subsequent flights.

Education and Training

Airplane dispatchers must have at least two years of college education with studies in meteorology or air transportation. Two years of work experience in air transportation may take the place of the college requirement. Airlines prefer to hire

EXPLORING

• Participate in flying clubs.

• Ask your librarian to help you find resources on airplanes and air traffic. Here are some suggestions:

Air Safety: Preventing Future Disasters by Timothy R. Gaffney (Enslow Publishers, Inc., 1999).

The Aircraft Encyclopedia by Roy Braybrook (Simon & Schuster, 1985).

Jane's Aircraft Recognition Guide by David Rendall (HarperCollins, 1999).

college graduates who have studied mathematics, physics, or meteorology.

There are a few schools around the country that offer dispatcher training. For information on these courses, contact the Airline Dispatchers Federation or visit its Web site. (See For More Info.)

Airplane dispatchers must be licensed by the Federal Aviation Administration. Airline dispatchers must be at least 23 years old and in good health. Your vision must be correctable to 20/20.

Earnings

Dispatcher salaries vary greatly among airlines. According to the Airline Dispatchers Federation, entry-level positions at smaller carriers pay about $20,000 a year. Senior dispatchers at major airlines earn more than $100,000 a year. In 1999, a few dispatchers earned close to $150,000 including overtime pay. Licensed dis-

TYPES OF AIRLINES

Airlines can be classified as international, domestic, regional, and all-cargo.

International airlines provide international service between major cities. Some of the most well known are Aeroflot-Russian International Airlines, Air Canada, Air France, American, British Airways, Delta, KLM (Netherlands), Lufthansa (Germany), Northwest (United States), SAS (Scandinavia), TransWorld (United States), and United (United States).

Domestic airlines provide service within a country. The largest domestic airlines in the United States are Continental, Southwest, and America West.

Regional airlines, or **commuter airlines,** concentrate their service in one area of a country. They specialize in "feeder" routes that provide service between small and big cities. U.S. regionals include Alaska, American Eagle, Mesa, and Atlantic Coast.

All-cargo airlines include Flight Express and Airborne Freight, and the air fleets of such companies as Federal Express and United Parcel Service.

patchers earn about $47,000 per year. Flight superintendents make up to about $52,800 per year, and shift chiefs, $66,000. Smaller airlines and air companies generally pay less, with some dispatchers earning as little as $8,000 per year.

Outlook

The larger airlines employ only about 1,000 dispatchers. Smaller airlines and some private firms also employ airplane dispatchers, but the number of dispatchers remains very small. The Airline Dispatchers Federation says the job market for dispatchers is currently good, especially with smaller commuter airlines.

Most major airlines consider dispatch positions as senior management level positions. Candidates are often selected from within the company after they have 15 to 20 years of experience in a variety of areas, including supervisory positions. Candidates selected from outside the company must have

FOR MORE INFO

For career books and information about high school student membership, national forums, and job fairs, contact:
Aviation Information Resources, Inc.
1001 Riverdale Court
Atlanta, GA 30337
800-AIR-APPS
http://www.airapps.com

Airline Dispatchers Federation
700 13th Street, NW, Suite 950
Washington, DC 20005
http://www.dispatcher.org

considerable experience at smaller carriers.

According to ADF, new graduates from dispatch schools should not expect to be hired by major airlines such as American, United, or Delta. A better choice would be to seek a position with a smaller carrier and get at least five years' experience before attempting to apply for a position with a major airline.

Automobile Service Technicians

Words to Learn

Carburetor: The device that mixes fuel and air and delivers the combustible mixture to the engine.

Chassis: The supporting framework of an automobile.

Cylinder: The tubular opening in which the piston moves up and down.

Motor: A device that converts electrical energy into mechanical energy.

Muffler: The noise-absorbing device through which exhaust gases pass.

Starter: The motor that cranks the engine to start it.

Transmission: The device that provides different gear ratios between the engine and wheels.

V-type engine: An engine with two banks of cylinders set at an angle to one another in the shape of a V.

What Automobile Service Technicians Do

Automobile service technicians, or *auto mechanics,* repair and service all kinds of automotive vehicles, such as cars, trucks, buses, and trailers. They find out why a vehicle is not running smoothly by running tests and looking for clues that show mechanical or electrical problems.

After locating the cause of the problem, the service technician makes the necessary repairs. If a part is too badly worn or damaged to be fixed, the service technician replaces it. Mechanics have to explain to the customer what is wrong with the vehicle, how it will be fixed, and the cost of labor and parts.

To keep cars and trucks from needing repairs in the first place, service technicians also provide preventive maintenance and tune-ups. They usually follow a checklist to be sure they don't overlook any important parts, such as belts, hoses, steering systems, spark plugs, brake systems, carburetors, and wheel bearings. Mechanics use many tools in their daily work, from simple hand tools to specialty and computerized tools.

Some workers specialize in only one type of vehicle and are known as bus, truck, motorcycle, or foreign-car mechanics. Others specialize in a type of repair, such as automatic transmissions, tune-ups, air-conditioning, brakes, radiators, or electrical systems. Service technicians may work in service stations, for new-car dealers, or for department stores with automotive service facilities. They may be employed by the federal, state, or local government, or for taxicab and auto leasing companies who repair their own vehicles.

Education and Training

Most employers prefer to hire service technicians to have at least a high school diploma. High school courses should include shop, especially auto mechanics, electricity, or electronics. As new cars become more computerized, mechanics will need technical skills to keep up with changing technology. Any classes in computer science will be helpful.

EXPLORING

• Many community centers offer general auto maintenance and mechanics workshops where you can practice working on real cars and learn from experienced instructors.

• Read trade magazines to learn what's new in the industry. You can find them at most public libraries or large bookstores.

• Many public television stations broadcast automobile maintenance and repair programs that can help beginners see how various types of cars differ.

• Ask a parent or older sibling to teach you how to change oil and tires, replace batteries and belts, and do other minor repairs.

BEGINNINGS

By the mid-1920s, the "Big Three" automobile makers—Ford, General Motors, and Chrysler—were producing millions of cars in America. With the combinations of bad roads and inexperienced drivers, accidents and breakdowns became common. People not only were unskilled in driving but had no idea how to maintain and repair their new machines. Suddenly there was a need for a new profession.

Already in 1899 the American Motor Company had opened a garage in New York and advertised "competent mechanics always on hand to make repairs when necessary." Gradually, other repair garages opened in larger cities, although they were few and far between. Automobiles were much simpler in the early years.

As cars became more complex, the need for qualified technicians grew. Dealerships began to hire mechanics to handle customer concerns and complaints. Gas stations also began to offer repair and maintenance services. By the 1950s, automobile service and repair garages were common throughout the United States.

Many vocational schools and community and junior colleges offer auto mechanics courses. In addition to training, mechanics must complete either an apprenticeship or an on-the-job training program. On-the-job training usually consists of three or four years of supervised work under the guidance of experienced service technicians. An apprenticeship also takes three to four years, and programs are offered through many auto dealers and independent repair shops. Specialized service technicians usually need additional training.

Auto service technicians can become certified by the National Institute for Automotive Service Excellence. Membership in a labor union may be a requirement for some mechanics.

Earnings

According to the U.S. Department of Labor, the lowest paid

automobile service technicians earned about $15,475 per year in 1998. The median salary for automobile service technicians was $27,370. Top paid technicians with experience and certification earned about $44,200 per year.

In many repair shops and dealerships, technicians can earn higher incomes by working on commission. In 1998, master technicians who worked on commissions earned between $70,000 and $100,000 a year. Employers often guarantee a minimum level of pay in addition to commissions.

FOR MORE INFO

Automotive Service Association
PO Box 929
Bedford, TX 76095-0929
800-272-7467
asainfo@asashop.org
http://www.asashop.org

National Automotive Technicians Education Foundation
13505 Dulles Technology Drive
Herndon, VA 20171-3421
703-713-0100
http://www.natef.org

For information on certification, contact:
National Institute for Automotive Service Excellence
13505 Dulles Technology Drive, Suite 2
Herndon, VA 20171-3421
877-273-8324
http://www.asecert.org

Outlook

Many new vehicles have on-board diagnostics (OBD) that detect both wear and failure for many parts and systems. Automobile mechanics need to stay current with such new technologies.

There are an estimated 189 million vehicles in operation today, so automobile service technicians should feel confident that there will be plenty of service and repair jobs. Skilled and highly trained technicians will be in particular demand. Less skilled workers will face tough competition. The government predicts the field will grow as fast as the average through 2008.

Automotive Industry Workers

Car Designs Recharged

Because of concern for the high cost and availability of gas, some car manufacturers have been thinking about other kinds of fuels for cars, such as electricity. Three manufacturers already sell electric-powered vehicles and other automakers are working on designs for electric automobiles.

Ford makes an electricity-fueled truck, the Ranger EV. It seats two to three passengers and can travel 60 to 80 miles on a charge. Honda's EV+ seats four and can travel 100 to 120 miles. GM's EV1 seats two and can travel 60 to 80 miles on a charge. Today, electric vehicles are limited in their use by the distance they can travel on a charge. However, as they become more popular, you may begin to see charging stations instead of gas stations along the road.

What Automotive Industry Workers Do

Automotive industry workers make automobiles in factories. They read instructions and assemble the parts. They also build, maintain, and operate machines and tools used to produce the parts.

Automotive industry workers work in different types of factories. Usually, the largest factories are called assembly plants, where the automobiles are assembled from parts shipped from factories all over the country. There are often several thousand workers employed at assembly plants. Smaller factories are called parts production plants. In these factories, workers produce a specific part or a group of parts, such as the steering wheel. These factories may employ a few dozen people to several hundred. In both types of factories, workers often work in shifts because the plants operate 24 hours a day.

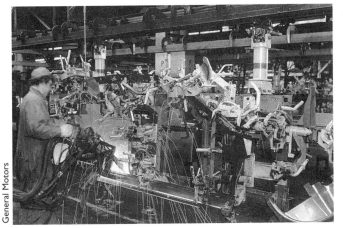

An auto industry employee works on an assembly line at a General Motors plant.

General Motors

Automotive workers work with their hands. They spend a lot of time standing, bending, and lifting, and they do a lot of repetitive work. They often work in noisy areas with heavy machinery and are required to wear safety gear, such as helmets, goggles, earplugs, gloves, and steel-toed shoes.

There are many types of jobs for automotive industry workers. *Machinists* operate the machines used to make automotive parts. They use tools, such as lathes, drill presses, and milling machines. *Tool and die makers,* or *precision metal workers,* design the tools, dies, and guiding and holding devices for machines. *Maintenance workers* set up new machines and repair and maintain them. *Supervisors* are experienced in production and are familiar with several machines and processes in their department. They supervise the

EXPLORING

• Take classes or find hobbies that involve working with your hands and building things from a number of small parts. Working on cars with a parent is ideal, but you can also learn from model-building or metalworking crafts.

• Learn to use power tools and hand tools.

• Tour a car assembly plant or a factory that manufactures parts.

HENRY FORD: AUTO INDUSTRY PIONEER

On January 14, 1914, Henry Ford raised the wages of his Ford Motor Company employees to an unheard of amount of $5 a day and cut the workday to eight hours. Then he decided to earmark $10 million of his company's $25-million-dollar earnings to an employee profit-sharing plan. His critics went wild. This will ruin the industry, they cried! We'll all have to pay workers more! But Ford remained undaunted. "I like to see folks who work hard get their fair share," he said in response. He believed the higher wages would boost worker loyalty and increase production.

To remain a Ford employee, however, the workers had certain standards they had to abide by. For one, they had to live in a comfortable house and were forbidden to take in a large number of boarders, a common practice for making additional income in Ford's day. Workers had to prove they were saving their money and often had to report how they were spending it. Ford became so demanding about how he wanted his employees to live their lives, he sent inspectors out to their homes. If you didn't follow the rules, you were fired.

production workers who produce the parts or assemble the cars. *Inspectors* make sure the parts meet specifications and that the metal used for the parts is high quality. *Welders* and *cutters* use equipment that joins metal parts by melting and fusing them to form a permanent bond.

Education and Training

Most jobs in the automotive industry require only a high school diploma. However, there is often strong competition for jobs with large automakers because they offer good benefits and pay. Therefore, if you have more training after high school, you stand a better chance of getting hired. Training in auto mechanics, electronics, welding, or drafting is helpful. Mathematics, including geometry, is useful for workers who may have to read blueprints. Community colleges and vocational-technical institutes offer one- or two-year programs in machining, welding, and toolmaking. These programs often include on-the-job training through internships or apprenticeships.

Earnings

Pay for semiskilled or unskilled workers, such as assemblers, is usually in the $20,000 range. Median annual earnings for welders in 1997 were $24,700 a year. Median earnings for machinists were $28,300. Earnings are usually much higher for workers who are members of a union and employed by a major automaker. Few of these workers earn less than $40,000 a year, and some earn as much as $100,000 a year because of overtime and six- or seven-day workweeks. Supervisors may earn $40,000 to $50,000 a year or more.

Outlook

In 1998, 756,700 workers were employed in the auto industry, according to the U.S. Bureau of Labor Statistics.

FOR MORE INFO

National Tooling and Machining Association
9300 Livingston Road
Fort Washington, MD 20744
800-248-NTMA
http://www.ntma.org

United Auto Workers
8000 East Jefferson
Detroit, MI 48214
313-926-5000
http://www.uaw.org

American Welding Society
550 Northwest Lejeune Road
Miami, FL 33126-5699
800-443-9353
http://www.aws.org

Most experts believe car sales will fall in the next few years. The drop in sales could cause production slowdowns and possible layoffs for auto industry workers, particularly those who work for American manufacturers. Today, however, many U.S. automotive workers are employed by foreign-owned automakers such as Honda and Mitsubishi.

Avionics Technicians

Words to Learn

Altimeter: A unit that measures the pressure outside an aircraft to determine the plane's altitude.

Distance measuring equipment (DME): Equipment used to determine the plane's distance from a particular station.

Radar: A unit that consists of a radio transmitter and receiver that emits radio waves and processes the reflections.

Radar altimeter: This unit measures the aircraft's distance above the ground by using radio signals that bounce off the ground.

Squawk: A complaint regarding a piece of equipment that is not functioning properly.

Transponder: A unit on a plane that receives signals sent from airports and replies back with a code that identifies the aircraft.

Voltmeter: An instrument that measures the differences, in volts, between various points of an electrical circuit.

What Avionics Technicians Do

When pilots fly a plane, they navigate, monitor the instruments, and communicate with air traffic controllers during the flight. They rely on radios, navigational equipment, autopilots, flight recorders, and other electronic equipment to help them fly safely. *Avionics technicians* make sure this equipment is in top working condition.

Avionics technicians install, repair, test, and service electronic equipment used in aircraft and spacecraft. After installing new systems, they test and calibrate the equipment to make sure it meets specifications set by the manufacturer and the Federal Aviation Administration (FAA). They adjust the frequencies of radio units and other communications equipment by signaling ground stations and making adjustments until the desired frequency is set. Avionics technicians also perform preventive maintenance checks so equipment will perform effectively.

Avionics technicians adjust and repair airplane parts.

Avionics technicians may work in a shop on individual pieces of equipment or outdoors on large aircraft. To comply with FAA rules, they keep detailed records and log all repairs and parts they replace. They use equipment and tools such as oscilloscopes, voltmeters, circuit analyzers, and signal generators to test and evaluate parts that need repair.

Technicians may help design and develop new electronic equipment. They consider operating conditions, including weight limitations, resistance to physical shock, atmospheric conditions the device will have to withstand, magnetic field interference, and other factors.

EXPLORING

• Join clubs or organizations involved with electronics. An amateur radio club will familiarize you with radio operation, frequencies, and some federal regulations.

• Work on science projects that focus on electronics, problem-solving skills, and your ability to build and fix things.

Technicians can specialize in radio equipment, radar, or flight-control systems. Because the field is always changing and growing, technicians must keep learning about new advances by reading technical articles and by taking classes.

Avionics is a term that comes from two words—aviation and electronics—and it refers to the use of electronics in the operation of aircraft, spacecraft, and missiles.

Education and Training

Avionics technicians need a solid background in advanced mathematics classes. Shop classes in electronics will be helpful.

You need some postsecondary training to obtain the basic skills you need to be an avionics technician. Some community colleges and technical schools offer one- or two-year programs in avionics that can lead to associate's degrees or certificates of completion. Some of the FAA-certified trade schools also have four-year programs in avionics or aviation technology. If an avionics program or course is not available in your area, you should take classes in electronics or earn an associate's degree in electronics. Some large corporations, especially those in the aerospace industry, have their own schools and training facilities. The U.S. armed forces also provide training in avionics and electronics.

AVIATION ON THE WEB

AVweb.com
http://www.avweb.com
Visit this Web site to read aviation news, reviews, training links, up-to-the-minute articles on new aircraft, and more.

NASA for Kids
http://kids.msfc.nasa.gov/Rockets/Airplanes

Earnings

Avionics technicians earned about $38,000 a year in 1998. Beginning technicians earn $18,000 to $20,000 a year. Salaries range from $25,000 to $50,000 a year for those with some experience. Federal government employees (not including armed forces personnel) on the average earn slightly less than avionics technicians employed by private aerospace firms.

Outlook

Since 1989, the aerospace industry has cut nearly 500,000 jobs. In 1994 alone, nearly 80,000 jobs were lost across the aerospace industry. Avionics, however, is still an important and constantly developing field that will continue to need more trained technicians. According to the U.S. Department of Labor, the job outlook is positive for avionics technicians and aircraft mechanics. Opportunities will be best at FAA-certified repair stations and smaller airlines. There will also be opportunities in small avionics repair shops that serve private citizens and businesses that own planes.

FOR MORE INFO

Contact the following organization for information on avionics careers:

General Aviation Manufacturers Association
1400 K Street, NW, Suite 801
Washington, DC 20005
202-393-1500
http://www.generalaviation.org/main.shtml

For information on careers, lists of schools, and scholarships, contact:

National Air Transportation Association
4226 King Street
Alexandria, VA 22302
703-845-9000
http://www.nata-online.org

Aerospace Industries Association of America
1250 Eye Street, NW, Suite 1200
Washington, DC 20005-3922
202-371-8400
http://www.aia-aerospace.org

Bicycle Mechanics

Bumpy Beginnings

The bicycle's ancestor was the *célérifere,* which appeared in Paris about 1790. It was a two-wheeled vehicle that the rider propelled by striking his feet along the ground.

The first practical mechanical bicycle was the *velocipede.* It was introduced by Pierre Michaux and Pierre Lallement about 1860. Its pedals were attached to the front axle and the front wheel was made larger than the rear to increase speed. The rider sat over the front wheel, which was as large as 60 inches in diameter. The velocipede's ride was so rough that it was quickly nicknamed "the bone shaker."

The safety bicycle appeared in 1879. It was designed by H. J. Lawson and improved upon in 1885 by J. K. Starley, both Englishmen. Starley's model was basically the same as the modern bicycle.

What Bicycle Mechanics Do

Bicycle mechanics work on both new and used bicycles. They do emergency repairs or routine tune-ups, or they may repair and recondition used bikes so they can be sold.

Repairing bicycles takes mechanical skill and careful attention to detail. Many repairs, such as replacing brake cables, are relatively simple, while others can be very complicated. There are many different brands of bikes, both domestic and foreign, and each has its own unique characteristics and mechanical problems.

Bicycle mechanics straighten bent frames using a special vise and a heavy steel rod. They adjust or replace braking mechanisms so that the force on the tire rims is spread evenly. They take apart, clean, grease, and reassemble the headset, or front hub, and the bottom bracket that houses the axle of the pedal crank.

The gear mechanism on multiple-speed bikes is another common repair for bicycle mechanics. On some bikes, gears are shifted by means of a derailleur, which is located on the back wheel hub or at the bottom bracket assembly where the pedals and chain meet. The derailleur moves the chain from one gear wheel to another and frequently needs adjustment. Gear mechanisms vary greatly among different makes of bicycles so mechanics have to keep up with current models and trends.

Many new bikes come from the manufacturer unassembled, and mechanics working at a bicycle dealership or shop must assemble them and make adjustments so they operate properly.

Mechanics who work in bike shops sometimes work as salespeople, advising customers on their bike purchases or biking accessories. In some shops, especially those located in resort areas, bike mechanics may also work as bicycle-rental clerks.

Education and Training

There are no special education requirements for bicycle mechanics, although employers usually prefer to hire high school graduates. Vocational-technical

EXPLORING

• Many people become interested in bicycle repair because they own and maintain their own bikes. Taking general maintenance and tune-up classes at a bike shop is a good way to explore your interest in working with bikes.

• Read cycling magazines. They often have regular features on the technical aspects of how bicycles are constructed and operated.

• You may find a biking club in your area to join. You will meet other biking enthusiasts and you may be able to attend workshops on bike repair.

A BIKE ISN'T JUST A BIKE

The **conventional bicycle** has a steel frame, a coaster brake, and wide, low-pressure tires. It usually does not have a gear system.

The **road bike** is lightweight and has thin, high-pressure tires. Most road bikes have drop-style (downturned) handlebars, hand brakes, and a 10- or 12-speed gear system with shift levers on the bicycle frame.

The **mountain bike** or **all-terrain bicycle** (ATB) has a sturdy frame and wide, low-pressure tires with a knobby tread for good traction. Most mountain bikes have straight handlebars, hand brakes, and a 15- or 18-speed gear system with shift levers on the handlebars. The saddle is usually wider than a road bike's and the rider sits in a more upright position.

The **hybrid bicycle,** also known as the **cross bike** or **fitness bike,** has a sturdy frame and seat similar to that of a mountain bike, but has thinner, higher-pressure tires.

The **high riser bicycle** has a small frame, upswept handlebars, and a high saddle. It has small wheels, usually 20 inches or less in diameter. High risers may have hand brakes, coaster brakes, or both. Most types have gear systems.

The **track bicycle** is used mostly on bicycle race tracks. It is very lightweight and has no gears or brakes.

The **recumbent bicycle** has a long frame with a low, chairlike seat. Its pedals are operated with the legs extended forward, rather than downward.

The **tandem bicycle** has two or more seats, sets of pedals, and handlebars, arranged one behind the other on the same frame.

and physics classes are helpful in this job.

Bicycle maintenance courses are offered at some technical and vocational schools, as well as a few private training schools. These schools usually award a certificate upon completion. Some bicycle manufacturers may offer factory instruction to mechanics employed by the company's authorized dealers. Generally, however, bike mechanics learn informally on the job. At least two years of hands-on training and experience are required to become a thoroughly skilled mechanic. Because new makes and models of bikes are constantly being introduced, additional and ongoing training may be required.

Earnings

Trainee mechanics, with less than one year's experience, start at minimum wage ($5.15 an hour). As they gain more experience and become more valuable to their employers, mechanics may earn $8 to $9 an hour. According to the U.S. Department of Labor, mechanics who also have sales responsibilities had an annual income of about $25,220 a year in 1998.

Outlook

Cycling continues to be popular. People are bicycling for fun, fitness, as a means of transportation, and for the thrill of racing. Bikes don't burn gas or pollute the atmosphere, and they are relatively cheap. With personal fitness and the preservation of the environment as two of our society's biggest concerns, the long-term bike sales curve is rising. The U.S. Department of Labor predicts employment for bicycle mechanics will grow faster than the average through 2008.

FOR MORE INFO

Barnett Bicycle Institute
2755 Ore Mill Drive, Suite 14
Colorado Springs, CO 80904
719-632-5173
http://www.bbinstitute.com

The Midwest Bicycle Dealers Association sponsors a Bicycle Service School. The Web site also contains employment information.
CABDA Midwest
2417 West 183rd Street
Homewood, IL 60430
708-798-2004
http://www.cabda.com

United Bicycle Institute
PO Box 128
Ashland, OR 97520
541-488-1121
http://www.bikeschool.com

Diesel Mechanics

The Good...

- The fuel used by most diesels is a light oil derived from petroleum. It is much less explosive than gasoline and therefore is safer to store and handle.

- Diesel engines are up to 50 percent more efficient than gasoline engines designed for comparable purposes. This means greater fuel economy for the diesel.

- The diesel is more ruggedly built and runs at lower speeds than most gasoline engines, so the engine is durable and has a long life.

- Compared with the steam engine, the diesel is smaller, lighter, more efficient, and needs less maintenance.

...and the Bad

- The diesel engine has to be of heavier construction to withstand added heat and stress, so it costs more to build and repair.

What Diesel Mechanics Do

Diesel mechanics work on the diesel engines that power buses, ships, automobiles, trucks, locomotives, construction machinery, and farm and highway equipment. Their work can be divided into three basic categories: maintenance, repair, and rebuilding.

Maintenance work is the day-to-day servicing that keeps the engine running smoothly. Mechanics check oil levels, the brake system, steering mechanisms, and wheel bearings. They clean air and oil filters, remove and check the various parts of the fuel system, and inspect the water cooling system.

Despite regular maintenance checks, parts of the engine can wear out or break. When this happens, mechanics remove, replace, and adjust the defective parts.

To rebuild an engine a diesel mechanic must take it completely apart. This is usually scheduled at regular intervals such as every 18 months or 100,000 miles. Mechanics use a variety of instruments to check parts and then they repair, adjust, or replace them.

Diesel mechanics work with heavy tools such as welding and flame-cutting equipment, power wrenches, and lathes and grinding machines. Most diesel mechanics work on the engines of heavy trucks, such as those used in hauling freight over long distances. All mechanics must know the principles of diesel engines and must be prepared to do exacting, often strenuous work to keep engines in good working order. They usually work indoors and are exposed to dirt and grease. Minor cuts and bruises on the hands are the most common injuries that diesel mechanics suffer.

Education and Training

Entry-level diesel mechanics need a high school diploma and some additional formal training. Training can vary from on-the-job or apprenticeships to formal classroom work in a technical or vocational school that offers courses in diesel equipment. Because of the time and money it

EXPLORING

• Many community centers offer general auto maintenance workshops where you can practice working on real cars with an instructor.

• Read trade magazines such as *Landline* and *Overdrive* to learn about the trucking industry.

• This Web site has basic information on how diesel engines work:

How Stuff Works
http://www.
howstuffworks.com/
diesel.htm

takes to train an apprentice, most employers today prefer to hire only those who have some postsecondary training.

Some firms, particularly those that manufacture diesel engines, offer their own formal training programs, which can last anywhere from six months to four years. The National Automotive Technicians Education Foundation offers voluntary certification through many technical schools. Diesel mechanics also need a Class A driver's license.

Earnings

Diesel mechanics' earnings vary depending upon their region, industry (trucking, construction, railroad), and other factors. According to the U.S. Department of Labor, the median pay for all diesel mechanics in 1998 was $14.11 an hour. Wages ranged from $9.36 to $20.78 an hour. Beginning mechanics usually start at 50 to 75 percent of skilled workers' wages and receive increases as they become more skilled. Many diesel mechanics belong to unions. Mechanics who work for companies that must operate

PROFILE: RUDOLF DIESEL (1858-1913)

The diesel engine was invented by German engineer Rudolf Diesel. Born in France in 1858, Diesel began his career as a refrigeration engineer. He had an idea for an engine that was more adaptable in size and less costly than the steam engine. It took him 13 years working in his laboratory in Paris to develop his engine. Diesel's engine design was based on the second law of thermodynamics—by raising the temperature of pure air to a very high degree when the engine's piston was beginning to descend, fuel could be introduced at precise amounts. Thus this new engine was very energy-efficient. Diesel's first engine blew up and nearly killed him, but proved that the principle was practical. His years of hard work paid off and his first successful engine was built in 1894.

around the clock, such as bus lines, may work at night, on weekends, or on holidays and receive extra pay for this work.

Outlook

The increase in diesel-powered vehicles, together with an increase in the use of trucks for cargo transportation, will create jobs for highly skilled diesel mechanics. Less skilled workers will face strong competition. The U.S. Department of Labor predicts employment growth to be about as fast as the average in the next 10 years.

The most jobs for diesel mechanics will open up at trucking companies who hire mechanics to maintain and repair their fleets. Construction companies are also expected to need more diesel mechanics to maintain their heavy machinery, such as cranes, earthmovers, and other diesel powered equipment.

FOR MORE INFO

Automotive Service Association
PO Box 929
Bedford, TX 76095-0929
800-272-7467
asainfo@asashop.org
http://www.asashop.org

United Automobile, Aerospace and Agricultural Implement Workers of America
8000 East Jefferson Avenue
Detroit, MI 48214
http://www.uaw.org

National Automotive Technicians Education Foundation
13505 Dulles Technology Drive
Herndon, VA 20171-3421
http://www.natef.org

National Institute for Automotive Service Excellence
13505 Dulles Technology Drive, Suite 2
Herndon, VA 20171-3421
703-713-3800
http://www.asecert.org

RELATED JOBS

Automobile Collision Repairers
Automobile Sales Workers
Automobile Service Technicians
Automotive Industry Workers

Industrial Traffic Managers

What Industrial Traffic Managers Do

Industrial traffic managers are in charge of transporting the goods their companies produce, as well as distributing goods within their own companies. These goods may include raw products such as grains, fruits, or livestock; manufactured goods such as tractors or safety pins; or piped liquids such as crude oil.

Traffic managers have to consider the type and quantity of the items to be shipped. Is the item liquid, bulky, light, heavy, or fragile? Does it catch fire easily, or would it release dangerous fumes if it were accidentally spilled? Managers design or select the containers the goods will be shipped in. Sometimes they are responsible for the actual packing of goods.

Industrial traffic managers must find the quickest, most economical way of shipping the goods. This could be by highway, rail, air, water, or pipeline. Managers approve bills, trace lost shipments, lease port or terminal facilities, or clear international goods through customs. They manage the shipping and receiving clerks who work under them, and also work closely with senior company officials to develop and establish transportation policies for the entire company. Because of the thousands of federal, state, and local regulations governing transportation, traffic managers must be familiar with the legal matters that concern their company's shipping.

Independent industrial traffic managers, or *logistics experts,* contract their services to one or more companies. They arrange for the storage and inventory control of parts or finished products and get them transported among manufacturers or between manufacturers and consumers.

Education and Training

Industrial traffic managers must have at least a high school diploma. It is recommended that you earn a college degree in business administration, transportation, or marketing. Some commercial law training will help you cope with complex rates, regulations, routes, and schedules.

EXPLORING

• To find out more about industrial traffic management, read these publications on the Web:

Logistics World
http://www.
logisticsworld.com

Freight World
http://www.
freightworld.com

• This Web site has transportation and logistics links for you to explore:
http://www.loglink.com

Many people interested in becoming traffic managers begin in the shipping room or general traffic offices of large plants. Those with more education will probably spend less time at beginning jobs, but experience and demonstrated ability are usually the most important factors in promotion to higher-level jobs.

To gain access to better jobs, traffic managers should seek certified membership in the American Society of Transportation and Logistics. This requires work experience and passing an examination.

Earnings

Experienced traffic managers earn salaries between $41,300 and $61,600 a year. The most experienced industrial traffic managers with master's degrees in business can earn as much as $100,000 a year. Entry-level positions pay about $15,000 a year. Starting salaries depend on your education, college-coordinated experience, other relevant work experience, and the degree of responsibility of the position. Traffic agents and clerks can earn up to $25,000 or more a year.

STUDY TIME

College students in industrial traffic management programs might take courses like these:

History of Transportation

Regulation of Transportation

Transportation and Distribution

Logistics

Tracking Systems

Freight Loss and Damage Claims

Import/Export Transportation Management

Transportation of Hazardous Materials

International Traffic Management

Transportation Law and Regulations

Industrial Psychology

Outlook

The employment outlook for industrial traffic managers is expected to grow more slowly than the average through 2008, according to the U.S. Department of Labor.

Large and medium-sized companies are increasingly using computers to store and retrieve records. Computers are also used to operate conveyor systems, robotics, trucks, and scanners, eliminating the need for large numbers of workers. Traffic management can never be completely computerized, however. Workers will still be needed to check shipments before they go out and when they arrive.

Shipping, receiving, and traffic clerks held about 774,000 jobs in 1998. Almost two out of three agents and clerks are employed by retail or wholesale companies or manufacturing firms.

FOR MORE INFO

American Society of Transportation and Logistics
229 Peachtree Street, Suite 401
Atlanta, GA 30303
404-524-3555
http://www.astl.org

Warehousing Education and Research Council
1100 Jorie Boulevard, Suite 170
Oak Brook, IL 60523-4413
630-990-0001
http://www.werc.org

RELATED JOBS

Billing Clerks
Bookkeeping and Accounting Clerks
Cost Estimators
Customs Officials
Export-Import Specialists
Postal Clerks
Railroad Clerks
Reservation and Ticket Agents
Shipping and Receiving Managers and Clerks
Statistical Clerks

Locomotive Engineers

What Locomotive Engineers Do

Locomotive engineers are responsible for the safe and efficient operation of locomotives. Some engineers operate passenger trains and others run freight trains that carry coal, lumber, and other products.

Before beginning a trip, engineers review their orders, noting the train's destination and any scheduled stops along the way. They check the time they are expected to arrive at the various stops. For those trains carrying cargo, engineers must know where the cargo will be unloaded and if any additional cargo will be loaded along the route. Engineers also inspect the train's fuel supply, water supply, and communications radio to be sure it is operating properly.

Once a train is running, engineers control the train's speed and watch the track in case a signal marker or obstruction on the track requires some action. During the

Santa Fe Railroad

A locomotive engineer maneuvers a train into a station.

EXPLORING

• Join a model railroad club or a railroad historical society. There are some helpful Web links at http://www.trainweb.org/dsrg/club.htm to help you find one.

• Here are some reading suggestions:

The American Diesel Locomotive by Brian Solomon (Motorbook International, 2000).

Eyewitness: Train by John Coiley (DK Publishing, 2000).

Illustrated Encyclopedia of World Railway Locomotives by P. Ransom-Wallis, ed. (Dover Publications, 2000).

trip, they use controls, such as the throttle lever that regulates the engine's speed, the reverse lever, and brake valves. Other controls operated by the engineer include the horn, bell ringer, sander, deadman pedal, and a control switch to connect the control circuits to their source of power.

Engineers are in frequent contact with the conductor during a trip to make sure there are no problems anywhere on the train. At the end of the trip, engineers check on the condition of the locomotive, make minor adjustments if needed, and report any major repairs to the repair shop.

Yard engineers work in switchyards, where cars are hitched together to make

al achievements for locomotive engineers, but you still need to be a high school graduate. A strong math background is necessary for any engineering job.

To become a locomotive engineer, you must be in good physical condition with excellent eyesight and good hearing. Engineers must pass physical examinations on a regular basis. They also are required to take a drug screening test. You must be 21 years old and complete locomotive engineer training. Most locomotive engineers start out as brakemen or conductors, where they work and train for engineer positions in railroad-sponsored training certification programs. There are also several community col-

trains. Yard engineers operate locomotives when they are being moved after a trip, being prepared for a new trip, or being loaded or unloaded.

Education and Training

Training and experience are more important than education-

leges that offer associate's degree programs in railroad operation.

Earnings

Earnings for locomotive engineers are negotiated in union contracts. The earnings depend on the class of locomotive operated, the kind of service in which the engineer is employed, and the amount of seniority he or she has. According to 1997 figures from the National Railroad Labor Conference, annual earnings for engineers ranged from an average of $52,903 a year for yard freight engineers to $65,374 for passenger engineers.

According to the U.S. Department of Labor, locomotive engineers earned about $19.14 an hour in 1998. Wages ranged from less than $12.22 to more than $33.65 an hour.

Outlook

There are only about 33,000 locomotive engineers in the entire United States and it is

FOR MORE INFO

Association of American Railroads
50 F Street, NW
Washington, DC 20001
202-639-2100
http://www.aar.org

**Brotherhood of
Locomotive Engineers**
1370 Ontario Street, Mezzanine
Cleveland, OH 44114
216-241-2630
http://www.ble.org

expected that the number of job openings in this field will be limited in the future. However, while the U.S. Bureau of Labor Statistics predicts a decline for all other railroad transportation workers, it does expect some growth in the number of locomotive engineer positions. Locomotive engineers are essential to a train's operation and the position has not suffered the cuts that assistant engineers and brake operators have.

Marine Engineers

What Marine Engineers Do

Ships and other vessels are designed for many different uses. Some have special piping to carry oil or natural gas. Others carry vehicles such as cars and trucks. Still others cruise warm waters with hundreds of vacationers on board. Depending on its purpose, a ship may be powered by diesel, steam, gas, or nuclear power.

Marine engineers design and build the engines that power these ships. They work closely with naval architects who plan the frames and hulls. Together, they try to produce lighter ships that use less fuel and need less upkeep.

The machinery and equipment on ships include power plants, navigation equipment, radio and radar gear, and fire control and electric power systems, as well as systems for heating, air-conditioning, refrigeration, and the removal of salt from seawater.

All About Propellers

Projecting from a ship's hull are one or more propellers. There are two types in use today.

The **screw propeller** consists of two to six blades mounted on a hub attached to the end of a drive shaft projecting from the stern. As the drive shaft turns, the blades rotate to push the ship forward. When the rotational direction of the drive shaft is reversed, the blades rotate in the opposite direction, moving the vessel backward. A screw propeller with movable blades, called a **controllable-pitch propeller,** can be adjusted to move a vessel backward without reversing the motion of the drive shaft.

A **cycloidal propeller** consists of a number of vertical blades mounted around a ring on the bottom of a vessel. The blades can be adjusted so the propeller will move the vessel forward or backward, turn it to the left or right, or hold it stationary in a strong current or tide.

Once construction of the ship is finished, marine engineers sail on the vessel to test equipment and correct any problems. Marine engineers also test equipment, repair ships, and design equipment used on docks and in marine structures. Some marine engineers plan offshore platforms for oil drilling.

On merchant marine vessels, marine engineers operate, maintain, and repair propulsion engines, boilers, generators, pumps, and other machinery on the ship. These vessels usually have four engineering officers: a chief engineer and three assistant engineers. The assistants stand periodic watches to oversee the safe operation of engines and machinery.

Marine engineers work for a variety of employers. These include private shipbuilders and naval architecture and marine engineering design firms. They also work for the various branches and agencies of the federal government.

Education and Training

If you are interested in marine engineering, you need to study math, including geometry, trigonometry, and calculus. Physics and chemistry classes are recommended, as well as courses in computer-

EXPLORING

• For U.S. Department of Transportation links to U.S. shipyards, see http://www.marad.dot.gov/nmrec/links/usshipyardsa.html.

• Tour a shipyard or visit a Coast Guard ship when it is open to the public.

• Books on shipbuilding and careers in water transportation are available at public libraries.

• The Propeller Club of the United States has an Adopt-A-Ship Program that allows classrooms to adopt a merchant marine ship. During the year, the students and ship's crew correspond and share experiences. For information, see http://www.americansteamship.com/adopt_a_ship.html.

aided design and mechanical drawing.

To design engines and machinery, marine engineers need at least a bachelor's degree in engineering. A master's degree or even a doctorate may be required for some jobs. This is especially true of jobs in teaching, research, and management.

You must be licensed to work on a merchant marine vessel. To qualify for an engineering officer's license, you must graduate from the U.S. Merchant Marine Academy or one of the six state academies and pass a written examination. The academies offer a four-year academic program leading to a bachelor of science degree, a license as a third assistant engineer (engineering officer) issued by the U.S. Coast Guard, and a commission in the U.S. Naval or Coast Guard Reserve.

WORDS TO LEARN

Beam: The width of the vessel at its widest point.

Bow: The forward end of the vessel.

Bulkhead: Vertical surfaces in the vessel much like walls in a house.

Bulwarks: The raised portion of the sides of a vessel around the main deck.

Cleat: A fitting of wood or metal with two horns used for securing lines.

Galley: The area on a vessel containing the cooking facilities.

Helm: The steering mechanism of a vessel.

Keel: The continuous section of a vessel running from the bow to the stern on which the vessel is built; the backbone of the vessel.

Leeward: The side of the vessel opposite the side where the wind is blowing.

Port: The left side of a vessel when facing forward.

Sheer: The curvature of a ship's deck from bow to stern.

Starboard: The right side of a vessel when facing forward.

Stern: The back end of a vessel.

Windward: The side of the vessel towards which the wind is blowing.

Earnings

The average annual salary for marine engineers is $40,200, according to the U.S. Department of Labor. Starting salaries for marine engineers with a bachelor's degree are about $30,000 in private industry. Government marine engineers can earn from $20,000 to $80,000 depending on their education and experience.

Outlook

Competition for marine engineering jobs has been strong. Military and commercial shipbuilding has been reduced in recent years, but more and more shipyards are building cruise ships, excursion/dinner boats, emergency and law enforcement craft, petroleum barges, and various double-hull vessels to meet the requirements of the Oil Pollution Act of 1990.

Employment in deep sea shipping has declined sharply because U.S.-staffed ships carry a smaller proportion of interna-

tional cargo. However, the number of vessels on the Great Lakes and on rivers and canals in the United States that carry bulk products, such as coal and grain, has increased and is expected to grow.

FOR MORE INFO

American Society of Naval Engineers
1452 Duke Street
Alexandria, VA 22314-3458
http://www.navalengineers.org

Society of Naval Architects and Marine Engineers
601 Pavonia Avenue
Jersey City, NJ 07306
http://www.sname.org

RELATED JOBS

Aircraft Mechanics
Avionics Engineers
Diesel Mechanics
Electronics Engineers
Marine Services Technicians
Mechanical Engineers
Military Workers

Marine Services Technicians

Iceberg Not Guilty in Titanic Case

What really caused the Titanic to sink? Contrary to popular belief, the iceberg was not directly responsible. Cold water temperatures—about 35 degrees Fahrenheit—caused the vessel's steel to crack like glass. During the first half of the 20th century, such brittle cracking reactions occurred in temperatures below 50 degrees Fahrenheit. During World War II, the government built more than 5,000 warships with the same flaw and more than 1,000 of them suffered similar failures. It wasn't until 1947, when a ship literally cracked in two in the cold water of Boston Harbor, that the problem was taken seriously. In 1963, the first definitive study was published by researchers at the U.S. Naval Research Laboratory describing the cracking problem in steel. Most of the world, however, continues to blame the iceberg.

What Marine Services Technicians Do

Marine services technicians inspect, maintain, and repair marine vessels, from small boats to yachts. They test and repair boat engines, transmissions, propellers; masts, rigging, and sails; navigational equipment; and steering gear. They repair or replace defective parts and make new parts to meet special needs. Technicians inspect and replace internal cabinets, refrigeration systems, electrical systems and equipment, sanitation facilities, hardware, and trim.

Marine services technicians with specialized skills may have more specific job titles. *Motorboat mechanics* work on inboard, outboard, and inboard/outboard engines. They perform routine maintenance tasks such as lubrication, cleaning, and adjusting parts. They use specialized equipment, such as engine analyzers, ammeters, voltmeters, and compression gauges, to diagnose engine problems.

Mathew Hohmann

A technician examines a motorboat engine for mechanical, fuel, and electrical problems.

EXPLORING

• Read trade magazines, such as *Professional Boatbuilder, Marine Mechanics,* and *Boating Industry.*

• If friends, neighbors, or relatives have boats, take trips with them and learn how to operate a boat. Offer to help do repairs to the boat, or at least watch someone do repairs and routine maintenance. Clean up the deck, sand an old section of the hull, or polish the brass. If a boat just isn't available to you, try to find some type of engine to work on. Even working on an automobile engine will help you understand what this type of work is like.

Motorboat workers also often install and repair electronics, sanitation, and air-conditioning systems.

Marine electronics technicians work with vessels' electronic safety and navigational equipment, such as radar, depth sounders, autopilots, and compass systems. They install, repair, and calibrate equipment and perform routine maintenance procedures such as checking, cleaning, repairing, and replacing parts.

Some technicians work on vessel hulls only. Hulls are usually made of wood or fiberglass. The hulls of most pleasure boats are built with fiberglass. Technicians reinforce damaged areas of the hull, grind damaged pieces with a sander, or cut them away with a jigsaw and replace them using resin-impregnated fiberglass cloth. They finish the repaired sections by sanding, painting them with a gel-coat substance, and buffing them.

Education and Training

Many marine services technicians learn their trade on the job. They find entry-level positions as general boatyard workers, doing such jobs as cleaning boat bottoms. Other technicians get more formal training at vocational or technical schools learning skills like engine repair and fiberglass work.

Some schools, such as Northwest Technical College in Minnesota and Cape Fear Community College in North Carolina, have associate's degree programs for marine technicians. Other institutions, such as the American

WORDS TO LEARN

Ammeter: An instrument that measures electric current.
Gyro compass: A type of compass using a continually spinning gyroscope so that the compass always points to the true north.
Inboard: An engine that is permanently mounted inside the hull of a boat.
Inboard/outboard (I/O): An engine that is mounted inboard but the propeller fits on an assembly that resembles an outboard motor drive (also called stern-drive). It is found in most speedboats and in other boat types that have high-power requirements.
Ohmmeter: An instrument that indicates electrical resistance.
Oscilloscope: An electronic instrument that graphically displays an electrical signal as a glowing line on a fluorescent screen. The pattern on the screen is actually a rapidly moving point of light.
Outboard: An engine mounted outside the hull of the boat, usually at the stern.

Boatbuilders and Repairers Association and the Wooden Boat School, offer skills training in less formal courses and seminars. These classes last days or a few weeks.

Marine services technicians who test and repair radio transmitting equipment must have a general radiotelephone operator license from the Federal Communications Commission. Certification for electronics technicians is voluntary and is offered by the National Marine Electronics Association.

FOR MORE INFO

For more information about a career as a marine services technician, contact:
Marine Retail Association of America
150 East Huron Street, Suite 802
Chicago, IL 60611
312-944-5080
http://www.mraa.com

For information on certification, the industry, and membership, contact:
National Marine Electronics Association
PO Box 3435
New Bern, NC 28564-3435
252-638-2626
http://www.nmea.org

Earnings

According to the U.S. Department of Labor, the median yearly earnings for small engine mechanics (including boat mechanics) were $21,580 in 1998. Salaries ranged from $13,400 a year to $32,800 a year. The 1998 edition of *The O*Net Dictionary of Occupational Titles* reports an average yearly income of $27,612 for marine services technicians.

Outlook

According to the U.S. Department of Labor, employment opportunities for small engine mechanics, including marine services technicians, are expected to grow slower than the average through 2008. As boat design and construction become more complicated, the outlook will be best for well-trained technicians.

Pilots

What Pilots Do

Airplane pilots and *helicopter pilots* operate aircraft. They transport passengers, freight, and mail and perform other commercial duties. The best-known pilots are commercial airline pilots, who fly for large airlines. They are in command of their crew, the plane, and the passengers during the time the plane is in motion on the runway and in the air.

Pilots first check the weather, flight conditions, and the flight plan, which is approved by the Federal Aviation Administration (FAA) and air traffic control personnel. On board a plane the pilot and *copilot,* who assists the pilot, test the instruments, controls, and electronic and mechanical systems. The pilot then gets orders from a dispatcher and taxis the plane (drives it at a slow speed along the ground) to a runway. There the pilot asks for permission to take off.

Much of the time the plane is in the air it is flown by an electronic device called an

A copilot sits at the instrument panel, preparing her plane for takeoff.

automatic pilot. The pilot and copilots continue to make radio reports to the ground, checking altitude, speed, weather conditions, and other details. Before landing, the pilot rechecks landing gear and requests landing clearance from air traffic controllers. When weather conditions are poor and the crew cannot see the runway, the captain may have to land the plane guided only by the plane's landing instruments.

There are many other kinds of pilots. *Agricultural pilots* spray crops to control insects and weeds, and to fertilize. These pilots are experts at flying but they must also understand the work of the farmers. Helicopter pilots transport passengers

EXPLORING

Learn to operate a ham radio. One of the qualifications for commercial flying is ham radio operation. There are many clubs that hold meetings and classes to teach the basic skills of radio operation and prepare you for your ham radio license test. You will find more information at this Web site: http://www.howstuffworks.com/hamradio3.htm or contact American Radio Relay League, 225 Main Street, Newington, CT 06111; 800-32NEW HAM.

WHAT DO HELICOPTER PILOTS DO?

Helicopter pilots work in medical evacuation, police and fire-fighting work, forestry, construction, communications, agriculture, and offshore oil exploration. They carry workers and supplies to oil rigs, rescue stranded flood victims, lift heavy materials to work sites, fly patients from one hospital to another, or give news and traffic updates for the media. Helicopter pilots who do police work are sometimes law enforcement officers as well. Their work includes traffic regulation and survey, vehicle pursuits, surveillance, patrol, and search.

During flight, helicopter pilots monitor dials and gauges to make sure the aircraft is working properly. They watch for changes in pressure, fuel, and temperature. They navigate using landmarks, compasses, maps, and radio equipment. In addition to flying, helicopter pilots keep records of their aircraft's engine performance and file flight plans. Before and after flying, they check the aircraft for problems and may even do repairs and general upkeep on the craft if they are licensed to do so.

Education and Training: Some helicopter pilots receive training in flying schools where, in addition to flight training, they study the theory of flying, weather, radio, navigation, and FAA Regulations. Many helicopter pilots learn to fly as officers in the army. A military pilot must pass the FAA military competency exam to become licensed as a commercial helicopter pilot.

Earnings: Commercial helicopter pilots make $33,700 to $59,900 a year. Corporate helicopter pilots earn $47,000 to $72,500 a year.

Outlook: The future of the helicopter industry is fair to good, growing by about 5 percent a year. Helicopters are being used more and more by police, fire, and rescue departments and in other fields and industries.

from jet airports to city centers. Helicopters are also used in rescue service, sightseeing, conservation service, traffic reporting, and aerial photography.

Education and Training

Many airlines require that their trainees be college graduates.

You will need to study meteorology, algebra, geometry, and mechanical drawing.

Pilots must meet strict training requirements, especially to work for commercial airlines. After flight instruction, you must pass a written exam and accumulate 250 hours of flying time.

Then you can apply for a commercial airline pilot's license. To receive this license, you must pass a physical exam and a written exam given by the FAA. Then you can apply for a copilot's position with an airline. Airlines have their own requirements, which often include up to 1,000 hours of flight time.

Earnings

The average starting salary for airline pilots is $15,000 a year at small turboprop airlines and $26,500 at larger airlines. With six years of experience, pilots can earn $28,000 at turboprop airlines and $76,000 a year at large airlines. Senior captains on the largest aircraft earn $200,000 a year. Agricultural pilots who work throughout the entire year can make between $30,000 and $80,000 a year.

Outlook

Employment for pilots will grow more slowly than the average through 2008. There is a lot of competition for pilot jobs. Many

FOR MORE INFO

Contact the following organizations for information on a career as a pilot:
Air Line Pilots Association, International
1625 Massachusetts Avenue, NW
Washington, DC 20036
703-689-2270
http://www.alpa.org

Federal Aviation Administration
800 Independence Avenue, SW
Washington, DC 20591
http://www.faa.gov

military pilots have had to enter the civilian workforce because of budget reductions in the U.S. military. Also, the high pay, prestige, and travel benefits make this a popular career choice for a growing number of people.

Employment opportunities for experienced agricultural pilots are expected to continue into the future, but these opportunities depend on farmers' needs.

Public Transportation Operators

A Bit of History

The first subway system, initially four miles long, was opened in London in the 1860s. The railcars were powered by steam until 1890, when the system was converted to electricity. New York, Chicago, Paris, Budapest, and many other cities followed with their own subway systems. Streetcar, or trolley, lines and elevated tracks were also built around this time. The first electric-powered elevated train system opened in Chicago in 1895.

The 20th century began with a new vehicle for public transportation: the gasoline-powered bus. Various cities throughout the United States established bus services in the first decade of the century. The first buses were trucks fitted with seats and automobiles lengthened for increased seating capacity.

What Public Transportation Operators Do

Public transportation operators transport passengers from one location to another by bus, subway, and streetcar. *Bus drivers* operate buses along a route and follow a regular schedule. Intercity bus drivers take passengers from one city to another, and local transit bus drivers transport passengers within a city. Others drive school buses, airport buses, or tour buses.

Local transit bus drivers usually make stops every block or two along their route. They may check passengers' identification cards, give information about schedules and routes, and collect fares. Intercity bus drivers also pick up and drop off passengers, collect fares, and answer questions. They may have to help in collecting and loading luggage, as well. Most bus drivers have to drive on weekends and holidays and at night.

Mathew Hohmann

A bus driver transports hundreds of passengers across town every day.

Subway drivers and other local railway system drivers have many of the same duties as bus drivers. They drive trains that transport passengers throughout cities and suburbs. They usually sit in special compartments at the front of the train where they operate it, starting, slowing, and stopping the train. Rail system drivers obey the signals along their routes, which run underground, at surface levels, or elevated above ground.

Some drivers announce stops over a loudspeaker, open and close doors, and make sure passengers do not get caught in the closing doors. Other drivers are assisted by agents, who collect fares and transfers,

EXPLORING

Get to know your city's bus and rail systems. Explore the public transportation systems of other cities. These Web sites will link you to information and maps for subway systems around the world:

MetroPlanet
http://www.metropla. net/index.htm

Subway Navigator
http://www. subwaynavigator.com

4 Subways
http://www.4subways. com

open and close doors, and announce stops. When trains malfunction or emergencies occur, drivers contact dispatchers and may have to evacuate passengers from the train cars.

Education and Training

To be a public transportation operator, you need to have a high school diploma. You must be in good health, have good eyesight, a good driving record, and no criminal record.

Federal regulations require bus drivers to have a commercial, or chauffeur's, license. The U.S. Department of Transportation requires that intercity bus drivers be at least 21 years old and some bus companies hire only drivers that are at least 24 years old. Specific requirements for local bus drivers and rail system operators vary by city.

Earnings

Earnings for public local transportation operators vary by location and experience. According to the U.S. Department of Labor, the 1998 median hourly wage for local and intercity bus drivers was $11.72. Wages ranged from $6.66 an hour to $19.18 an

WORLD'S LARGEST SUBWAY SYSTEMS

City	Date system completed	Number of riders in 1997 (in millions)	Length (km)
Moscow	1935	3,160	200+
Tokyo	1927	2,740	169.3
Mexico City	NA	1,420	178.0
Seoul	NA	1,390	NA
New York City	1904	1,130	320.0
Paris	1900	1,120	200.9
Osaka	1933	1,000	99.1
Hong Kong	NA	779	28.2
London	1863	770	391.0
São Paulo	NA	701	NA

NA = not available

hour. School bus drivers on average made less, with a median hourly wage of $9.05. Subway and streetcar operators averaged the highest median salary at $20.83 an hour.

According to 1999 data from the American Public Transit Association, local transit bus drivers in cities with more than 2 million people earned $17.90 an hour on average for companies with over 1,000 employees. Companies with less than 1,000 employees paid an average of $16 per hour. In smaller cities of 250,000 to 500,000, bus drivers earned an average of $14.70 an hour. They earned an average of $12.60 an hour in cities that had a population below 50,000.

Outlook

Employment for public transportation operators is expected to grow as fast as the average for all occupations through 2008, according to the U.S. Department of Labor. As the population increases, local and intercity travel increases. Future government efforts to reduce traffic and pollution through greater funding of public transportation could also improve job opportunities.

FOR MORE INFO

For transit news and links to local chapters, contact:
Amalgamated Transit Union
5025 Wisconsin Avenue, NW
Washington, DC 20016-4139
202-537-1645
http://www.atu.org

For salary statistics and other career information, contact:
American Public Transit Association
1666 K Street, NW
Washington, DC 20006
202-496-4889
http://www.apta.com

For information on careers in public transportation, contact:
Transport Workers Union of America
80 West End Avenue
New York, NY 10023
212-873-6000
http://www.twu.com

Railroad Conductors

The U.S. Railway Service

U.S. railways get more than 90 percent of their revenue from transportation of freight. The four major categories of freight are coal, chemicals, grain, and motor vehicles and equipment. Other products include petroleum, lumber, livestock, ore, coke, stone, and scrap materials.

There are two types of passenger service in the United States: intercity and commuter. The National Railroad Passenger Corporation (Amtrak) provides intercity service to major cities. In some of the larger cities—New York, Chicago, Boston, Philadelphia, San Francisco—there is commuter service providing transportation for workers to and from the central area of the city.

What Railroad Conductors Do

A *railroad conductor* is the person who yells "All aboard!" in movies and on television, but real-life conductors have much more responsibility than that. Conductors are in charge of the entire train, including other train employees and all the train equipment. On trains today, a conductor and the locomotive engineer may be the only two crew members aboard the train.

Some railroad conductors supervise trains that carry passengers and freight. They are called *road conductors. Yard conductors* work in rail yards, directing workers on switching crews that put together and take apart trains.

Conductors who work on freight trains keep track of each car's cargo. They make sure cars are dropped off or picked up at certain stops. They also inspect the cars to make sure that they are in good condition and properly sealed.

Conductors who work on passenger trains attend to the comfort and safety of passengers. They oversee the boarding of passengers, and collect tickets and fares. At stops, they help passengers get off the train safely, and tell the engineer when to pull away from the station. If there is an accident, conductors take charge of the situation.

On both passenger and freight trains, conductors are in constant contact with the locomotive engineer. Before departing, they go over schedules and times with the engineers. During the run, conductors may receive information over the radio about track conditions or special instructions. They may also monitor information about any problems with the train's operation and pass that information along to the engineer using a two-way radio. When working in rail yards, conductors make sure that trains are put together and ready to go on time. They throw switches to direct cars to certain tracks for unloading. They tell switching crews which cars to put together and which ones to take apart.

Education and Training

A high school education is required to enter this field. Machine shop and electrical shop classes are good choices for

EXPLORING

• The Federal Railroad Administration includes information on its Web site for students to learn more about railroads. Visit the site at http://www.fra.dot.gov.

• Join a club of railroad and train enthusiasts.

• For information on railroads, see this Web site:
Webville and Hypertext Railroad Company
http://www.spikesys.com/webville.html

RELATED JOBS

Locomotive Engineers
Public Transportation Operators
Railroad Clerks
Shipping and Receiving Managers and Clerks

RAILWAY MUSEUMS

The history of railroads continues to interest people of all ages even today—years after the railroad's heyday as the nation's chief means of transportation. Railway museums can be found all over the country and are a great way to get a feel for how much railroads affected the average American's life in the early 20th century. The Illinois Railway Museum, for example, boasts large collections of restored locomotives, passenger and freight trains, and streetcars. The museum is located in Union, Illinois, and bills itself as the largest railroad museum in the United States. Visitors can see locomotives and cars, as well as artifacts, such as buildings, signals, telegraph/communications, tools, signage, tickets, caps, and badges. Some unique cars and locomotives in the museum's collection include the Electroliner, the Nebraska Zephyr, the only remaining Chicago streamlined PCC streetcars, the first GP7 diesel engine, the only interurban sleeping car, and an 1859 horsecar.

On the West Coast, the Golden Gate Railroad Museum has a collection of cars and locomotives on the naval base at Hunter's Point, San Francisco. Its collection includes the Southern Pacific 2472, a steam locomotive built in 1921; the Atchison-Topeka-Santa Fe 2356 diesel locomotive built in 1948 by the American Locomotive Company; and passenger cars built in the 1920s by George Pullman.

future conductors. Computer science is also helpful.

Railroad conductor is not an entry-level job. Most conductors gain experience by working different jobs for the railroad and after years of experience are promoted to conductors. To be a conductor, you must be in good health. Most railroads require you to pass physical examinations before starting work and you must be able to lift at least 80 pounds.

Earnings

The average annual salary for yard-freight conductors is $48,991, according to 1997 National Railroad Labor Conference figures. Local-freight conductors averaged $62,169 a year. In 1998, one major railroad paid conductor trainees $300 to $400 a week, or about $16,000 a year. Once they became full-fledged conductors, they earned $28,496 annually for the first year. After the fifth year of being a conductor, earnings increased to $35,672.

According to the U.S. Department of Labor, median earnings of railroad conductors and yardmasters were $18.15 an hour in 1998. Wages ranged from less than $13.60 to more than $24.16 an hour.

Outlook

Job opportunities are not promising for railroad conductors. Rail passenger services to many points have been discontinued. Although the volume of railroad freight business is expected to increase in the coming years, the use of mechanization, automation, and larger, faster trains is expected to cause a continued decline in the employment of rail transportation workers.

Computers are now used to keep track of empty freight

FOR MORE INFO

For general information on the railroad industry, contact:
Association of American Railroads
50 F Street, NW
Washington, DC 20001
202-639-2555
http://www.aar.org

For information on the career of conductor, contact:
United Transportation Union
14600 Detroit Avenue
Cleveland, OH 44107
216-228-9400
http://www.utu.org

cars, match empty cars with the closest load, and dispatch trains. Also, new work rules that allow two- and three-person crews instead of the traditional five-person crews are becoming more widely used. These factors combine to lessen the need for conductors and other crew workers.

Reservation and Ticket Agents

Words to Learn

Booking: A reservation.

Coach: The economy class on an airline.

Computerized Reservation Systems (CRS): Computer systems that allow immediate access to fares, schedules, and availability. They can also be used to make reservations and buy tickets. The two most common ones are Sabre and Apollo.

Confirmation number: A code that identifies and documents a booking.

Layover: A stop on a trip, usually associated with a change of planes or other transportation.

Luxury class: The most expensive accommodations or fare category.

What Reservation and Ticket Agents Do

Reservation and ticket agents make and confirm travel arrangements for clients and prepare and sell tickets to customers. They help travelers plan their trips by answering questions about trip prices. They suggest what routes to take and when to begin and end a journey.

Reservation agents usually work in large offices answering telephone calls from customers and booking reservations. Most agents work for airlines, but the same procedures are followed by agents who work for bus, train, or other transportation companies. After they find out when and where the customer wants to go, reservation agents type instructions on a computer keyboard and quickly obtain information on flight, bus, or train schedules. If a plane is full, the agents may suggest an alternate flight or check to see if space is available on another airline that flies to the same location. After

American Airlines

Reservation and ticket agents handle the stream of calls that come in each day from travelers.

the travel reservation has been made and the ticket has been purchased, the tickets are sent to the passenger, or picked up at the time of travel.

Ticket agents sell tickets to customers at airports, bus terminals, and railway stations. They answer customer questions and may check baggage, examine visas or passports (if the passenger is traveling to a foreign country), ensure passenger seating, and direct passengers to the proper boarding areas. Ticket agents also keep records of the passengers departing on each trip.

EXPLORING

Ask your parents to let you help plan your next family vacation. You can:
- Help choose a location that interests all members of your family.
- Put together a notebook of information about the location you plan to visit. Check libraries and bookstore travel sections. Search Web sites. Send for brochures, maps, and other information from a city, state, or country's tourism office.
- Help figure out the best way to travel to your vacation spot. Use the Internet or the telephone to contact air, bus, and rail lines to find out prices and schedules.

U.S. BUREAU OF TRANSPORTATION STATISTICS 1998

- U.S. passengers logged 463,262,000 air travel miles, 148,325,000 miles by bus, and 5,304,000 miles by train.

- The average passenger air trip was 813 miles, the average bus trip was 144 miles, and the average rail trip was 252 miles.

- Passengers spent $97,662,000 on air travel, $1,738,000 on inter-city bus travel, and $5,709,000 on rail travel.

When flights or train or bus runs are delayed or canceled because of poor weather or other conditions, reservation and ticket agents must explain the situation to unhappy travelers and try to make other arrangements for them. Because the transportation industry operates 24 hours a day, reservation and ticket agents often work irregular hours, including evenings and weekends.

Education and Training

Although there are no specific educational requirements to become a reservation or ticket agent, most employers prefer to hire high school graduates with at least some college training. As the field becomes more competitive, a college degree will become increasingly important.

Reservation and ticket agents should be able to read and understand travel schedules and have some computer skills. Agents who speak a foreign language are always in great demand, as more and more international travel occurs each year.

All agents receive on-the-job training, during which they are taught how to read schedules, calculate fares, and make travel arrangements.

Earnings

According to the Economic Research Institute, average salaries for new agents were $20,176 in 1999. With six years of experience, they earned approximately $26,550. After 12 years, they earned an average of $31,790 a year. Railroad and bus companies tended to pay lower wages.

Outlook

According to the U.S. Department of Labor, demand for reservation and ticket agents is expected to grow more slowly than the average for all occupations through 2008. "Ticketless" travel, or automated reservations ticketing, is reducing the need for agents. In addition, many airports now have computerized kiosks that allow passengers to reserve and purchase tickets themselves.

FOR MORE INFO

For information on the airline industry, contact:
Federal Aviation Administration
800 Independence Avenue, SW
Washington, DC 20591
800-322-7873
http://www.faa.gov

For information on education, internship, scholarship, or certification in travel and tourism, contact:
National Tourism Foundation
546 East Main Street
PO Box 3071
Lexington, KY 40508
800-682-8886
http://www.ntfonline.com

Passengers can also access information about fares and flight times on the Internet, where they can also make reservations and purchase tickets. However, for security reasons, all of these services cannot be fully automated so the need for reservation and transportation ticket agents will never be completely eliminated.

Signal Mechanics

Signal Basics

Railroads use two types of signals. **Block signals** keep trains a safe distance apart by warning of trains or cars on the track ahead. **Interlocking signals** control the movement of trains through complex sections of track, such as at crossings, junctions, or drawbridges.

Each section of track, from signal to signal, is one block. Only one train is permitted in each block. A typical block length is about 2 to 3 miles.

A red signal means the next block is occupied. The train must stop to let another train or some other danger to pass. A yellow signal means that the next block is clear, but that the block following that is occupied or unsafe. If a train approaches a yellow signal, it means the signal following is red, so the train has the length of one block to stop. A green signal means that at least the next two blocks are clear.

What Signal Mechanics Do

Signal mechanics or *signal maintainers* are railroad employees who install, repair, and maintain the signals and signal equipment along railroad tracks. They inspect and test lights, circuits and wiring, crossing gates, and detection devices.

Signal equipment includes computerized and electronic equipment detection devices and electronic grade crossing protection. To install signals, workers travel with road crews to designated areas. They place electrical wires, create circuits, and construct railway-highway crossing signals, such as flashers and gates. When signal mechanics install new signals or signal equipment, they or other crew members may have to dig holes and pour concrete foundations for the new equipment, or they may install precast concrete foundations. Because railroad signal systems are sometimes installed in the same areas as underground fiber optic cables, signal mechanics must be familiar with marking systems and take great care in digging.

Signal mechanics who perform routine maintenance are generally responsible for a specified length of track. They are often part of a team of several signal mechanics, called a signal construction gang. They drive a truck along the track route, stopping to inspect and test crossings, signal lights, interlock equipment, and detection devices. When servicing battery-operated equipment, they check batteries, refill them with water, or replace them with fresh ones if necessary. They use electrical testing devices to check signal circuits and wiring connections, and they replace any defective wiring, burned-out light bulbs, or broken colored lenses on light signals. They clean the lenses with a cloth and cleaning solution and lubricate moving parts on swinging signal arms and crossing gates. They tighten loose bolts, and open and close crossing gates to make sure that the circuits and connections in the gates are working.

Sometimes signal mechanics are sent to make repairs in response to reports from other rail workers about damaged or malfunctioning equipment. In these cases, the

EXPLORING

• These magazines have general railroad industry news:

Railway Age
http://www.railwayage.com

Trains
http://www.trains.com

• To learn more about railroad signals, visit these Web sites:

How to Read Railroad Signals
http://members.nbci.com/amrail/vebdoc13.htm

Railroad Signals
http://home.pacbell.net/jimn61vi/rrsignals.html

mechanic analyzes the problem, repairs it, and checks to make sure that the equipment is functioning properly.

EARLY SIGNALS

Railroad signals were developed to let train crews know about conditions on the track ahead of them. Signaling systems became necessary in the 19th century when early steam-driven trains began to operate so fast that they presented the danger of collision with one another.

The first attempt to avoid accidents was a timetable system. This system was based on running trains on timed schedules, so that there was always a space between them. However, if a train broke down, the next train's crew had to be informed somehow so that it could react appropriately. In 1837, on a rail line in England, a telegraph system was introduced in which signals were sent on telegraph wires between stations up and down the tracks. The track was divided into blocks, or sections, with a signalman responsible for each block. As trains passed through the blocks, one signalman telegraphed messages to the next block, allowing the next signalman to decide whether it was safe for the train to proceed through that block.

Education and Training

Signal mechanics need mechanical aptitude and a firm knowledge of electricity. Railroads require new job applicants to pass written tests that cover AC/DC electronics.

You must have at least a high school diploma to be a signal mechanic. Some railroads require applicants to have college degrees in electronics or electrical engineering. Other railroads will consider applicants who have military experience in electronics, or who have a two-year degree in electronics from a technical school.

Workers are usually trained both on the job and in the classroom. Some of the biggest railroads have their own schools. For example, Norfolk Southern sends its signal trainees to its training center in McDonough, Georgia, where they study electrical and electronics theory; signal apparatus, protection devices, and circuits; federal railroad administration policies; and signaling procedures.

Earnings

According to the U.S. Department of Labor, signal maintainers had a yearly income of $32,136 in 1998. In the fall of 2000, Norfolk Southern reported that signal maintainers had a starting salary of about $15.75 an hour (about $32,760 for full-time employment). Assistant signal workers earned about $14.35 an hour ($29,850 annually) to start. Signal shop foremen earn about $37,428 a year. Signal gang foremen earned $34,848 and assistant signal foremen earned $33,456 a year.

Outlook

The U.S. Department of Labor predicts employment for most railroad transportation occupations, including signal mechan-

FOR MORE INFO

For general information on the railroad industry, contact:
Association of American Railroads
50 F Street, NW
Washington, DC 20001
202-639-2100
http://www.aar.org

For information on the career of railroad signal mechanic, contact:
Brotherhood of Railroad Signalmen
PO Box U
Mount Prospect, IL 60056
847-439-3732
signalman@brs.org
http://www.brs.org

ics, will decline through 2008. There will be few new job openings, and competition for existing positions is expected to be quite strong because of the good pay and high job security and satisfaction. Signal maintainers with the strongest technical training will be in the greatest demand in the coming years.

Toll Collectors

What Toll Collectors Do

Toll collectors receive payments from motorists and commercial drivers for the use of highways, tunnels, bridges, or ferries. The U.S. economy depends on the huge web of roads, bridges, and tunnels that spreads across the country. This transportation system allows people to travel from state to state, workers to get to and from work, and goods to get from farms to factories to stores. Because the cost of building and maintaining the system is high, many roads, bridges, tunnels, and ferry boats charge a fee, or toll, to the people who use them.

Toll collectors perform a wide range of duties. They collect fees from vehicles passing through toll stations. The rates vary according to the size or weight of the vehicle. Collectors make change, count and sort the money they receive, fill out bank deposit slips, and keep written records on the amount of traffic and kinds of vehicles that pass their stations.

Toll collectors receive payment from drivers who use toll bridges or roads.

Toll collectors also give directions to travelers, pass on messages received through their radio equipment, and contact state police, ambulances, or other emergency services when necessary. They are responsible for closing down a traffic lane when necessary to allow emergency vehicles to pass through without stopping. Toll collectors monitor the automatic lanes (the exact-change lanes where motorists toss their toll money into a basket) and electronic-pass lanes. They check for unsafe or prohibited vehicles on the roadway, and make sure the equipment at their station is working properly.

EXPLORING

If you are interested in toll collecting, contact state and local departments of transportation, as well as state highway departments. School counselors may have additional information on tollway careers or related agencies to contact about the nature of the job and its requirements.

HISTORY LESSON

Throughout history, the upkeep and maintenance of roads around the world usually fell to the reigning powers. However, in 1663, three counties in England obtained authority to levy tolls on users to pay for the improvement of a major road linking York and London. By the 18th century, all major roads in Great Britain incorporated tolls, or turnpike trusts, to pay for maintenance.

In 1785, Virginia built a turnpike and other states quickly followed suit. The first hard-surfaced road of any great length in the United States was the Lancaster Turnpike, completed in 1794. Almost 150 years later, the first successful U.S. toll road for all types of motor vehicles was built, also in Virginia.

Toll booths are open around the clock, every day of the year. Collectors' busiest shifts are usually on holidays, evenings, and weekends.

Education and Training

Toll collectors need at least a high school education. Recommended high school courses include mathematics, speech, and English classes. Those who want to be managers should have some college experience as well. If you have worked as a cashier, you may have an advantage over other applicants, but no previous training is required. Any experience in handling money and making change is valuable. All collectors must take an exam before being hired. You are tested on your ability to deal with the public, make change, handle other financial transactions, and keep records and write reports.

Earnings

Toll collectors' salaries vary from state to state, but on the average, beginning toll collectors earn about $15,900 per year and increase to around

$28,000 with additional experience and a good employment record. Managerial responsibilities will also increase earnings. Part-time employees are usually paid by the hour and may begin at the minimum wage ($5.15 an hour). Toll collectors who are members of a union generally earn more than those who are not. Collectors who work the later shifts may also earn more, and most employees earn time-and-a-half or double-time for overtime or holiday work.

Outlook

Employment opportunities for toll collectors are in decline because of the use of electronic toll collection (ETC). The technology includes computerized systems that identify and classify vehicles, as well as capture video images of license plates that do not have a valid tag. Computerized toll-collecting is convenient for truck drivers and commuters who frequent the toll roads, but states that use ETC have put a freeze on hiring additional toll collectors or

FOR MORE INFO

Contact your state department of transportation for information on toll collector jobs. Additional information may be obtained from:

American Association of State Highway and Transportation Officials
444 North Capitol Street, NW, Suite 225
Washington, DC 20001
202-624-5800
http://www.transportation.org/aashto/home.nsf/FrontPage

International Bridge, Tunnel and Turnpike Association
2120 L Street, NW, Suite 305
Washington, DC 20037
202-659-4620
http://www.ibtta.org

replacing toll collectors who retire or move into other jobs. Still, a small number of toll collectors will be needed to collect tolls from drivers who do not participate in ETC. Toll collectors may need additional training to monitor and maintain this new technology.

Traffic Engineers

A Challenge for Traffic Engineers

Each year more than 3.8 million crashes occur at intersections that account for nearly 10,000 deaths, according to the National Highway Traffic Safety Administration. The Federal Highway Administration reports that in 1999, red-light running accidents caused 92,000 crashes leading to 90,000 injuries and 950 deaths. Between 1992 and 1998, deaths due to red-light running crashes totaled nearly 6,000. More than half of these deaths were pedestrians and occupants in other vehicles who were hit by the red-light runners. Another 2,779 deaths occurred in the vehicles running the red lights. In the same time period, about 1,500,000 people were injured in such crashes.

What Traffic Engineers Do

Traffic engineers work to increase road safety and to improve the flow of traffic. They study traffic conditions such as signal timing, traffic flow, high-accident zones, lighting, road capacity, and entrances and exits. In planning and creating their designs, engineers consider anything that might affect traffic, such as nearby shopping malls, railroads, airports, or factories. They apply standard mathematical formulas to certain measurements to compute traffic signal duration and speed limits. They prepare drawings showing the location of new signals or other traffic control devices. They may study changes in traffic conditions and sometimes recommend new traffic controls and regulations.

Traffic engineers address a variety of problems in their daily work. They may figure out a way to reduce the number of accidents on a particularly dangerous section of highway. They might prepare traffic impact studies for new residential or industrial developments, to make sure the roads are equipped to handle the increase of traffic. To do this they may recommend adjusting the timing of traffic signals, widening lanes, or creating bus or carpool lanes. Traffic engineers also have to be aware of the effect their recommendations will have on nearby pedestrian traffic and environmental concerns, such as air quality, noise pollution, and the presence of wetlands or other protected areas.

Traffic engineers who work in government often design or oversee roads or entire public transportation systems. They might manage the design, planning, and construction of new roads and highways or monitor a system that controls the traffic signals by the use of a computer.

Education and Training

Traffic engineers must have a bachelor's degree in civil, electrical, mechanical, or chemical engineering. Because the field of transportation is so vast, many engineers have educational backgrounds in science, urban planning, computers, and environmental planning.

EXPLORING

Study the traffic in your town or neighborhood. Make a map that shows traffic patterns. Mark traffic signals, stop signs, and one-way streets. On busy streets, mark exits and entrances to shopping centers and other businesses. Note areas that have the highest pedestrian traffic. What are the speed limits? What are the times of the day or week when traffic is heaviest? Which intersections or roads have the highest accident rates?

RELATED JOBS

City Managers
Civil Engineers
Civil Engineering Technicians
Industrial Engineering Technicians
Industrial Traffic Managers
Statistical Clerks
Statisticians
Urban and Regional Planners

Traffic engineers acquire some of their skills through on-the-job experience and through training conferences and mini-courses offered by employers, educational facilities, and professional engineering societies. The Institute of Transportation Engineers offers Professional Traffic Operations Engineer certification. Traffic engineers should enjoy solving problems. They need good oral and written communication skills since they frequently work as part of a team. Engineers must also be creative and be able to visualize the outcome of their plans.

Earnings

According to a salary survey by the Institute of Transportation Engineers, entry-level junior traffic engineers (Level I) earn starting salaries of $34,772 a year. Level II traffic engineers, with a minimum of two year's experience and who oversee small projects, earn $41,318 a year. Level III engineers, who supervise others and organize small to mid-size projects, earn $51,563 a year. Level IV engineers, who are

10 MOST DANGEROUS INTERSECTIONS

The State Farm Insurance Companies have named these intersections as the most dangerous in the country:

1. Flamingo Road and Pines Boulevard, Pembroke Pines, FL
2. Red Lion Road and Roosevelt Boulevard, Philadelphia, PA
3. Grant Avenue and Roosevelt Boulevard, Philadelphia, PA
4. 7th Street and Bell Road, Phoenix, AZ
5. 51st Street and Memorial Drive, Tulsa, OK
6. 71st Street and Memorial Drive, Tulsa, OK
7. 19th Avenue and Northern Avenue, Phoenix, AZ
8. State Highway 121 and Preston Road, Frisco, TX
9. Clearview Parkway and Veterans Memorial Boulevard, Metairie, LA
10. Fair Oaks Boulevard and Howe Avenue, Sacramento, CA

To find the dangerous intersections in your state, according to State Farm, go to http://statefarm.com/media/danlist00.htm.

responsible for the supervision of large projects, staffing, and scheduling, earn annual salaries of $61,908. Those traffic engineers who have titles such as director of traffic engineering, director of transportation planning, professor, or vice president (Level V) earn average salaries of $72,867 a year. Level VI engineers who have advanced to upper-level management positions, such as president, general manager, director of transportation or public workers, and who are responsible for major decision-making, earn the highest salaries at $86,375 a year.

Outlook

There were nearly 24,000 traffic engineers in the United States in the 1990s. Employment for traffic engineers is expected to increase faster than the average through 2008. More engineers will be needed to work with ITS (Intelligent Transportation System) technology, such as electronic toll collection, cameras for traffic incidents/detec-

FOR MORE INFO

Institute of Transportation Engineers
1099 14th Street, NW, Suite 300 West
Washington, DC 20005-3438
202-289-0222
http://www.ite.org

**American Association of State
Highway and Transportation Officials**
444 North Capitol Street, NW, Suite 249
Washington, DC 20001
202-624-5800
http://www.transportation.org/aashto/
home.nsf/FrontPage

**American Public
Transportation Association**
1666 K Street, NW
Washington, DC 20006
202-898-4000
http://www.apta.com/

U.S. Department of Transportation
400 Seventh Street, SW
Washington, DC 20590
202-366-4000
http://www.dot.gov

tion, and fiber optics for use in variable message signs. As the population increases and continues to move to suburban areas, qualified traffic engineers will be needed to design traffic plans.

Truck Drivers

What Truck Drivers Do

Truck drivers drive trucks and vans over long and short distances and make deliveries from producers to customers. *Long distance drivers*, also known as *over-the-road drivers*, transport goods in diesel-powered tractor-trailers. They often drive from state to state and might go cross-country, frequently driving at night. Long distance drivers must be able to maneuver their huge trailers around loading docks, inspect their trucks before and after long trips, and keep a daily log.

Two types of employers hire truck drivers: private and for-hire carriers. Private carriers include grocery store chains and large manufacturing plants that pick up and deliver their own goods. For-hire carriers are trucking firms that make deliveries for any company that hires them. Drivers who work for hire may own their own trucks, or they may lease them.

Delivery drivers, also known as *route-sales drivers,* drive vehicles to deliver merchandise within a limited area. These local drivers often drive small trucks or vans within specified neighborhoods delivering goods such as bread, soft drinks, and ice cream to stores. They often collect payments from the stores they deliver to, and may have to set up merchandise on shelves. Some drivers also try to sell customers new products or find new customers on their route.

Both truck drivers and delivery drivers may be expected to make minor repairs to their vehicles to keep them in good working order. These workers also must be very skilled drivers because they have to maneuver their trucks through congested city traffic, fit their vehicles into tight parking spaces, and sometimes drive through narrow alleys.

Drivers sometimes load and unload their own vehicles. Drivers of heavy trucks (over three tons) generally have a helper who assists with loading and unloading. Drivers of moving vans usually have a crew of helpers. Some heavy-truck drivers operate special vehicles, including dump trucks, oil trucks, and cement-mixing trucks.

EXPLORING

These two online magazines provide a look at issues in the trucking industry and a list of answers for frequently asked questions for people interested in trucking careers:

Overdrive
http://www.etrucker.
net/overdrive/index.htm

Land Line
http://www.
landlinemag.com

RELATED JOBS

Industrial Traffic Managers
Public Transportation Operators
Taxi Drivers
Toll Collectors
Traffic Engineers

Education and Training

High school courses in driver training and automobile mechanics are good preparation for this career. Bookkeeping and business courses will teach you skills for keeping accurate records of customer transactions.

Truck drivers must have a good driving record. Most employers of delivery drivers provide on-the-job training. Most trucking companies prefer to hire drivers who are at least 21 years old. Employees must pass physical exams that check vision, use of arms and legs, and blood pressure. Some drivers must be able to lift heavy objects.

Many drivers work with little supervision, so they need to be mature and responsible. In jobs where drivers deal directly

NO-ZONE CAMPAIGN

Safety is a major concern for truck drivers and also for the drivers they share the road with. That's why the Federal Highway Administration launched a campaign to educate other drivers about truck drivers' blind spots and how to avoid them.

No-zones are the danger areas around commercial vehicles where crashes are more likely to occur. For example, a truck has a much larger blind spot on both of its sides than a car. When other drivers drive in these no-zones for any length of time, they can't be seen by truck drivers. Also, when cars cut in too soon after passing, then abruptly slow down, truck drivers are forced to compensate with little time or room to spare.

Many trucks carry signs on the back that warn other drivers of wide right turns. Truck drivers sometimes need to swing wide to the left in order to safely negotiate a right turn. Rear blind spots are also a problem because trucks, unlike cars, have deep blind spots directly behind them. A truck driver can't see cars in this position and the car driver's view of traffic is also severely reduced.

Generally speaking, the bigger the truck, the bigger its blindspots, the more room it needs to maneuver, the longer it takes to stop, the longer it takes to pass it, and the more likely the car will be the loser in a collision.

with company customers, it is important for drivers to be pleasant, courteous, and able to communicate well with people.

Earnings

Over-the-road truck drivers are paid a cents-per-mile rate. Most companies pay between 20 and 30 cents per mile, but large companies are advertising higher rates to attract good drivers. J. B. Hunt, for example, the nation's largest publicly held trucking company, advertised 37 to 40 cents per mile to start in early 1999. At that rate, based on a weekly average of 2,500 miles, a driver would earn $925 to $1,000 a week.

Tractor-trailer drivers usually have the highest earnings and their average hourly pay generally increases with the size of the truck. The annual earnings of long-distance drivers can range from about $20,000 to well over $40,000. Owner-operators have average earnings between $20,000 and $25,000 a year. Although some local truck

FOR MORE INFO

American Trucking Associations
Office of Public Affairs
2200 Mill Road
Alexandria, VA 22314-4677
http://www.trucking.org

Professional Truck Driver Institute of America
2200 Mill Road
Alexandria, VA 22314
http://www.ptdia.org

drivers are guaranteed minimum or weekly wages, most are paid an hourly wage and receive extra compensation for overtime work.

Outlook

The employment of truck drivers is expected to increase about as fast as the average rate through 2008. Currently, there is a shortage of both local and over-the-road drivers. The U.S. Department of Labor predicts that about 507,000 new truck drivers will be hired between 1998 and 2008.

Glossary

accredited: Approved as meeting established standards for providing good training and education. This approval is usually given by an independent organization of professionals to a school or a program in a school. Compare **certified** and **licensed**.

apprentice: A person who is learning a trade by working under the supervision of a skilled worker. Apprentices often receive classroom instruction in addition to their supervised practical experience.

apprenticeship: 1. A program for training apprentices (see apprentice). 2. The period of time when a person is an apprentice. In highly skilled trades, apprenticeships may last three or four years.

associate's degree: An academic rank or title granted by a community or junior college or similar institution to graduates of a two-year program of education beyond high school.

bachelor's degree: An academic rank or title given to a person who has completed a four-year program of study at a college or university. Also called an undergraduate degree or baccalaureate.

certified: Approved as meeting established requirements for skill, knowledge, and experience in a particular field. People are certified by the organization of professionals in their field. Compare **accredited** and **licensed**.

community college: A public two-year college, attended by students who do not live at the college. Graduates of a community college receive an associate degree and may transfer to a four-year college or university to complete a bachelor's degree. Compare **junior college** and **technical college**.

diploma: A certificate or document given by a school to show that a person has completed a course or has graduated from the school.

doctorate: An academic rank or title (the highest) granted by a graduate school to a person who has completed a two- to three-year program after having received a master's degree.

fringe benefit: A payment or benefit to an employee in addition to regular wages or salary. Examples of fringe benefits include a pension, a paid vacation, and health or life insurance.

graduate school: A school that people may attend after they have received their bachelor's degree. People who complete an educational program at a graduate school earn a master's degree or a doctorate.

intern: An advanced student (usually one with at least some college training) in a professional field who is employed in a job that is intended to provide supervised practical experience for the student.

internship: 1. The position or job of an intern (see intern). 2. The period of time when a person is an intern.

junior college: A two-year college that offers courses like those in the first half of a four-year college program. Graduates of a junior college usually receive an associate degree and may transfer to a four-year college or university to complete a bachelor's degree. Compare **community college.**

liberal arts: The subjects covered by college courses that develop broad general knowledge rather than specific occupational skills. The liberal arts are often considered to include philosophy, literature and the arts, history, language, and some courses in the social sciences and natural sciences.

licensed: Having formal permission from the proper authority to carry out an activity that would be illegal without that permission. For example, a person may be licensed to practice medicine or to drive a car. Compare **certified**.

major: (in college) The academic field in which a student specializes and receives a degree.

master's degree: An academic rank or title granted by a graduate school to a person who has completed a one- or two-year program after having received a bachelor's degree.

pension: An amount of money paid regularly by an employer to a former employee after he or she retires from working.

private: 1. Not owned or controlled by the government (such as private industry or a private employment agency). 2. Intended only for a particular person or group; not open to all (such as a private road or a private club).

public: 1. Provided or operated by the government (such as a public library). 2. Open and available to everyone (such as a public meeting).

regulatory: Having to do with the rules and laws for carrying out an activity. A regulatory agency, for example, is a government organization that sets up required procedures for how certain things should be done.

scholarship: A gift of money to a student to help the student pay for further education.

social studies: Courses of study (such as civics, geography, and history) that deal with how human societies work.

starting salary: Salary paid to a newly hired employee. The starting salary is usually a smaller amount than is paid to a more experienced worker.

technical college: A private or public college offering two- or four-year programs in technical subjects. Technical colleges offer courses in both general and technical subjects and award associate degrees and bachelor's degrees.

technician: A worker with specialized practical training in a mechanical or scientific subject who works under the supervision of scientists, engineers, or other professionals. Technicians typically receive two years of college-level education after high school.

technologist: A worker in a mechanical or scientific field with more training than a technician. Technologists typically must have between two and four years of college-level education after high school.

undergraduate: A student at a college or university who has not yet received a degree.

undergraduate degree: See **bachelor's degree**.

union: An organization whose members are workers in a particular industry or company. The union works to gain better wages, benefits, and working conditions for its members. Also called a labor union or trade union.

vocational school: A public or private school that offers training in one or more skills or trades. Compare **technical college**.

wage: Money that is paid in return for work done, especially money paid on the basis of the number of hours or days worked.

Index of Job Titles

agents, 59, 66-69
agricultural pilots, 55, 57
air traffic controllers, **6-9**, 14
aircraft mechanics, **10-13**, 29
airframe mechanics, 12
airplane dispatchers, **14-17**
arrival controllers, 6
assemblers, 25
automobile mechanics, 18-21
automobile service technicians, **18-21**
automotive industry workers, **22-25**
avionics technicians, **26-29**

bicycle mechanics, **30-33**
bus drivers, 58-61

conductors, 62-65
copilots, 55
cutters, 24

delivery drivers, 83, 84
departure controllers, 6
diesel mechanics, **34-37**
director of traffic engineering, 81
director of transportation, 81
director of transportation planning, 81
dispatchers, 14-17

en route controllers, 9
en route specialists, 6
engineers
    locomotive, 42-45, 63

marine, 46-49
traffic, 78-81
yard, 43, 44

flight data and clearance delivery specialists, 6
flight superintendents, 14-17

ground controllers, 6, 7

helicopter pilots, 54, 55, 56

industrial traffic managers, **38-41**
inspectors, 24

line mechanics, 10
local controllers, 6
locomotive engineers, **42-45**, 63
logistics experts, 39
long distance drivers, 82, 85

machinists, 23
maintenance workers, 23
marine electronics technicians, 51
marine engineers, **46-49**
marine services technicians, **50-53**
mechanics
    aircraft, 10-13
    airframe, 12
    automobile, 18-21
    bicycle, 30-33
    diesel, 34-37
    line, 10

motorboat, 50
overhaul, 11, 12
signal, 70-73
small engine, 53
motorboat mechanics, 50

naval architects, 46

overhaul mechanics, 11, 12
over-the-road truck drivers,
  82-85

pilots, 6, 8, 14, 15, **54-57**
precision metal workers, 23
public transportation operators,
  58-61

rail system operators, 60
rail transportation workers, 65
railroad conductors, **62-65**
railroad transportation workers,
  45
reservation agents, 66-69
reservation and ticket agents,
  66-69
road conductors, 62
route-sales drivers, 83

shipping and receiving clerks,
  39
shipping, receiving, and traffic
  clerks, 41

signal gang foremen, 73
signal maintainers, 70-73
signal mechanics, **70-73**
signal shop foremen, 73
small engine mechanics, 53
subway and streetcar operators,
  58-61
subway drivers, 59
supervisors, 23, 25

technicians
  automobile service, 18-21
  avionics, 26-29
  marine electronics, 51
  marine services, 50-53
ticket agents, 66-69
toll collectors, **74-77**
tool and die makers, 23
tractor-trailer drivers, 85
traffic agents and clerks, 40
traffic engineers, **78-81**
truck drivers, **82-85**

welders, 24

yard conductors, 62
yard engineers, 43, 44
yard-freight conductors, 64
yardmasters, 65

Transportation on the Web

Association of American Railroads

http://www.aar.org

Bureau of Transportation Statistics

http://www.bts.gov/edu

Federal Aviation Administration

http://www.faa.gov

Federal Railroad Administration

http://www.fra.dot.gov/site

How Airplanes Work

http://www.howstuffworks.com/airplane.htm

Maritime Administration

http://www.marad.dot.gov/kids/index.html

National Highway Traffic Safety Administration

http://www.nhtsa.dot.gov

National Transportation Safety Board

http://www.ntsb.gov

U.S. Department of Transportation

http://www.dot.gov